Exceptional

Exceptional

The Autobiography of Fletcher Johnson, MD, Heart
Surgeon, NCAA Star, NBA Pro, and Civil Rights Warrior

FLETCHER JOHNSON, MD
Compiled and Edited by Thomas Trzyna

RESOURCE *Publications* · Eugene, Oregon

EXCEPTIONAL
The Autobiography of Fletcher Johnson, MD, Heart Surgeon, NCAA Star, NBA
Pro, and Civil Rights Warrior

Resource Publications
An Imprint of Wipf and Stock Publishers
199 W. 8th Ave., Suite 3
Eugene, OR 97401

www.wipfandstock.com

PAPERBACK ISBN: 978-1-7252-6448-9
HARDCOVER ISBN: 978-1-7252-6449-6
EBOOK ISBN: 978-1-7252-6450-2

Manufactured in the U.S.A.   03/31/20

Contents

Preface

Born in 1931, Fletcher Johnson succumbed to pancreatic cancer in 2008, at the age of 77, leaving his wife Jeanne and their sons Jaime and Benjamin. Jeanne now works as a nurse specially accredited to work with deep and incurable wounds. Jaime is a company representative for a pacemaker manufacturer. After a career in banking, Ben is now an award-winning brew-master at the Philipsburg Brewery in Montana. Fletcher's son by his first marriage, Chino, was a camera man for Ted Koppel and continues to work in film. His daughter Renee is deceased. In spite of the terrible ordeal of the false charges brought against him and ten years of litigation, Fletcher built his medical mall, prospered in his practice, and was showered with accolades and awards. His marriage remained strong, and his children succeeded in their goals.

The skeleton of this autobiography was transcribed by Jeanne's sister Elin, who courageously worked with Fletcher's large spiral-bound notebooks that included a handwritten draft of his early life. Fletcher's handwriting is huge and sprawling. Other fragmentary drafts were transcribed from dictations by medical typists. The material he wrote and edited himself by hand is remarkable for its power, vocabulary, and sometimes amazing choices of words. There are sixteen separate fragments. The editor also consulted two published magazine interviews, basketball magazine notices, an essay on the speech that Adlai Stevenson autographed and gave to Fletcher, an essay Fletcher wrote as part of his work on the local school board, his curriculum vitae, some family correspondence, legal correspondence, and his medical thesis published in French. The objective from the start was to use Fletcher's own words and to compile and edit an autobiography, rather than to write a biography using additional sources from interviews and from the six large boxes of records he left. Some names have been changed to allow past conflicts to sleep. Our commitment was to let Fletcher speak and to re-spect all his values and viewpoints. With Jeanne's approval, the editor added chapter headings and about two pages of contextualizing, transitional, and emphasizing sentences. The editorial task chiefly consisted of organizing, deleting redundancies, and being vigilant to include every fresh anecdote and reflection from the many thematically and chronologically overlapping drafts. The drafts were woven together chronologically. Dr. Bill Purcell care-fully read the manuscript and corrected many names that were transcribed inaccurately.

The editor had the privilege of meeting Fletcher Johnson only twice, once in 1972 and again in about 1979. The editor's wife Martha was a good friend of Jeanne when she finished high school in South Pasadena, California. They have continued to be close. At our first meeting, Fletcher spoke about his intention to write an autobiography, and I offered what little help I could muster. Ten years after Fletcher's death, Jeanne was ready for someone to work with the drafts. That task has been a joy, an honor and a mission. My own career included some forty years of teaching American ethnic literatures at various colleges. I claim no expertise. However, I do not believe I have encountered a book as exceptional as this. Fletcher's early life reads like passages from Richard Wright. Toward the end of the book, he is a sophisticated and masterful entrepreneur and physician who faces a blunt racist attack by an institution afraid of open competition.

Fletcher builds on two themes to be found in every African American autobiography: the importance of hard work and of education as liberating forces. His story covers a transitional period for African America, from the 1930s through 1998, a period of oppression, activism, hope and disappoint-ment. He offers important insights into the integration of sports, into the challenges facing blacks who wished to practice medicine, into the politics of medical practice, and into his successful inter-racial marriage, which Jeanne and Fletcher sealed at a time when their choice was still highly con-troversial. His brief and challenging dialogue with Martin Luther King gives us a picture of views held by those who did not fully support non-violent change. Fletcher remained a strong believer in American exceptionalism, in spite of the racism he faced throughout his life. He also represents an impor-tant strain of African American religious conservatism. In the end, his story is framed by its first chapter. How does it continue to be possible for such a man, an NCAA star, an NBA pro, a multi-lingual European basketball phenomenon, a trained pharmacist, a European-educated heart surgeon, to come home to America after eight and half years of success to be met by people who saw him as nothing other than an example of the meanest word in their vocabulary? His capacity simply to survive his ordeals is stunning.

Fletcher Johnson's remarkable story deserves to be studied, to be analyzed and discussed, and to be taught in schools. It is inspiring for anyone who wants to rise, whether in sports, medicine or any other endeavor. He provides us with a detailed anatomy of institutional racism. His autobiography is strong testimony to the persistence of racism in America and to the extraordinary strength and courage that has enabled African Americans to contribute so richly and profoundly to every art, science and profession. We need to continue that "larger conversation" he recommends about race and equity.

Thomas Trzyna, Seattle, 2020.

Returning to America

The beginning. Whoever told you men were created equal was flat out wrong. Men never are equal, never have been equal, and never will be equal.

Granted, the means by which men are created are equal no matter what mystical, spiritual, faith-based system or lack of one you may believe in. The simple biological truth is that when an egg is penetrated by a sperm, a human being is created. This act is the same for all human beings. Once this act is completed, no human being is precisely like any other, one might say EQUAL. Genes, chromosomes, climate and socio-economic environments blend to make one individual different from another. Through these factors people become unequal in their intellect, physical appearance, physical strength, skills, talents, morals, priorities and their ability to adapt to the changing environment.

Boatloads of anthropologists will tell you that humanity started in deepest Africa, often dubbed the dark or black continent. The gradations of skin color had to do with the multiple mutations people had to undergo to survive the drastic climate and terrain changes they encountered as they migrated to the far corners of the Earth. I view the sun, the light of the world, as the great arbitrator in determining skin color and many of the other physical differences among the white, yellow, brown, red and black races. The closer one comes to the equator, the darker the skin. As one ventures further from the equator, the directness of the sun decreases and there is not the same need for protective pigments, and thus the skin becomes lighter. Consider the huge white polar bears of the North Pole and compare them to the large, black grizzly bears found in the USA. Regard the deer and their spring and summer coats which are tan to red, compared to the gray browns of wintertime that closely match the bare and leafless winter trees.

I can assure you that several inches inside the nose, mouth, vagina and rectum of a Japanese, Polynesian, Navajo, Swedish or Manhattan black, tissues are the same color—pink. Furthermore, open the chest cavity and the heart, lungs, esophagus, and thymus are the same color in every human race. The same goes for the abdominal cavity—the stomach, liver, spleen, kidneys and intestines large and small. Science has proven that a black man's heart can be transplanted and function in a white man. Successful organ transplant does not depend on the skin color of the donor or the recipient. No matter what your parents, teachers, preachers, rabbis or anyone else taught you to believe, the bare-knuckle truth is that skin color does not confer a superior intellect or greater physical prowess.

God, only God, could have made this day. The sky held a few scattered pearl-white glistening billowy columns of clouds against a magnificent baby blue background. The warm mid-day spring sun gave life to new grass and different hues of green to burgeoning new leaves on the trees bordering the New York Garden State Parkway. I had come from the Bronx and its prestigious Montefiore/Albert Einstein Medical complex on my way to an interview with Dean McKinnsey of Rutgers University. He was the chairman of the department of Cardio-Thoracic surgery. At that time I was, in all of the United States, one of four Americans of African descent who had been fully trained to be heart surgeons. My chief, George Robinson, was a world-renowned cardiac surgeon and had recommended me highly after my four-year surgical residency and a two-year fellowship with him in cardiac surgery. As I flowed along in my scarcely two-month old Citroen Maserati, golden with totally hand-fashioned black leather interior, I could hear the throaty sound of the Maserati engine and feel the featherbed softness of the Citroen air suspension as it smoothed the road.

I glided over the George Washington Bridge westward down route 4 and past the sign for Englewood, the city in which I had grown up. I had left on a basketball scholarship to Duquesne University in Pennsylvania, had become the best sixth man in college basketball, was drafted into the NBA by the Syracuse Nationals, earned my BA in Education, became a first lieutenant in the USAF, played eight and a half years of professional basketball in Italy and Switzerland, and had earned a degree in pharmacy in Italy and an MD in Switzerland, learning Italian and French as I studied. I had returned to the United States for six and a half years of training to become a cardiovascular, thoracic and general surgeon. Now, after some twenty-four years of perseverance and study after high school, going from professional basketball player to heart surgeon, I was finally ready to make a living as a doctor. Yet on this beautiful day, seeing the Englewood city sign, my mind drifted back to my days as a child when other children who all seemed to be high-yellow, light skinned, or at least lighter than me, would let me know I was nothing but a nigger. They let me know they saw me as a pug-nosed, thick-lipped, nappy-headed, raggedy-assed Johnson boy, whose mere appearance was an occasion for chanting: If you're white, you're right; If you're yellow, you're mellow; If you're brown, stick around; If you're black, git back, way back. There was just no way I could be their equal.

I remembered, too, coming back into this country after eight and a half years with an MD and a letter of recommendation, and an introduction to the chief of surgery at the Bellevue Hospital in NYC. I was sitting outside his door waiting for him when I heard the lady to whom I had given my letter say to someone, "Just wait until chief so and so sees that Nigger sitting out there with a letter recommending that he be appointed to an Internship." And when I was accepted as the first black intern at Englewood Hospital, in the town where I grew up, that presented such a problem for the hospital's education officer that he sent me off to Jersey City Medical Center for two months and posted a sign in the ER to warn Englewood that it was going to have its first Negro Intern, and it should be cleared with patients before I could examine them. A significant number of the black nurses were so unaccustomed to seeing a black doctor that they not infrequently called me Mr. or assigned me patients as if I were a private duty nurse. Sometimes they thought I was housekeeping and told me to make beds, help with lifting patients, or clean up broken glass. Then there was a black chef at the hospital, a long-time employee, who was brought in by ambulance in florid pulmonary edema. I was covering the ER for a Bergen County practitioner who was recovering from a stroke. I treated that chef with Lasix, morphine, oxygen, digitalis, sat him up, drew off a unit of blood, and he came out of heart failure immediately. As soon as he was able to speak, he said, "I don't want no Nigger doctor. I deserve a white doctor. I've been working here for over thirty years."

Englewood

Growing up was 90% misery and 10% longing to be grown.

My grandfather was traded for a horse at Fletcher's and Johnson's plantation in Kentucky. Since the dawn of time and certainly since Biblical times, slavery has played a part in every society known to man. There appear to be woven into the fabric of every single man the primordial, primitive, almost instinctive elements of competition, one-upmanship, envy, jealousy, and a holier-than-thou attitude. Such people have long been the cause of wars and are often fanatically tied to a religion that proclaimed themselves or their religion as the only one everyone should believe in or practice to the exclusion of all others—a total intolerance for any persuasion or religion outside their own or their own race. The vast majority of these zealots have this fanatic element as an integral part of their personality structure.

Slavery was born out of losing in battle. Associated with this attitude of "I am better than you and you are less than me" was people being captured and sold into slavery, though some people sold themselves into slavery to satisfy debts or to pay for passage to the USA. My grandparents, in their childhoods, were slaves. They were second generation slaves. At my grandmother's knee I learned about the human carnage and atrocities inherent in slavery. Members of my family were captured from coastal African villages, beaten, chained, stripped of all human decency. They were shipped chained to other slaves and to the benches in the bowels of slave ships.

My grandmother was our unending source of stories of this journey to America. Stories filled with horrors. She told of how slaves developed infected, gaping wounds from the chains themselves and the wooden benches or the decks to which they were chained and where they defecated and slept. The contaminated food they were occasionally fed was responsible for life-taking dysenteries. Any untoward moaning, movement, or discipline problems were meet with swift and severe beatings. The slave masters carried out these whippings and batterings. They tossed the dead slaves overboard, and if the provisions started to run out for the crew, they would throw overboard mid-ocean the sickest, the weakest, or the most problem-making among the slaves. The female slaves were raped by the crew whenever and wherever they pleased, often to a cheering, on-looking crowd. Survivors who reached America were placed on the slave block and sold to the highest bidder. The highest bids were for male, blue-gummed niggers, reputed to be the best field hands. Next were the females with bountiful breasts, good skin, and wide, large, child-bearing haunches. The slaves were treated as, inspected as, and bought as any other farm animal.

My paternal grandfather and his family were trained to raise, care for, and train racehorses. After the slaves were freed, my father's family, because of their skill and popularity with racehorses, became one of the wealthiest families in Columbia, South Carolina. In fact, my father, an only child, was the first person to have a Model T Ford in the whole town. Unfortunately, my grandfather was an alcoholic who beat my grandmother often. There came a day when my grandmother left a pasture gate open and one of his prize bulls cornered her in the barnyard. It was about to gore her to death when my father jumped in with a pitchfork, saving her by sticking the bull in the chest. The bull died instantaneously. My grandfather, however, was inconsolable about the death of his bull. He thought only of his prize bull, got drunk, and tried to beat up my father and grandmother. My dad saved her, and they fled to New Jersey. Several years later, my father sent for his beautiful sweetheart Edna, whom everyone called "sweet gal." She had been raised by her Uncle Tom when her parents died. Then my grandfather sent word that he was coming to take her home. He got off the train in Jersey City rather than Morristown, and he was killed by a mugger for the money he was carrying. No one was convicted of that murder. Grammy didn't know that anything was done to find that murderer. It was a case of niggers killing niggers, equaling no great loss. So Grammy continued to live with us, much to the chagrin of my mother, who wanted to run her own household.

Gramm butted into everything, telling mom how to raise us children, what to cook, what to wear, when and where to go to church, who her friends should be, who should be allowed to come to our home, how to clean house, who she should or should not wash and iron clothes for, and whose houses she should or should not clean. Gramm was a total trip. Her name was Sirlius. She stood nearly six feet tall, cursed like a sailor, and had clear skin that was a beautiful peach color. Her face was pretty, though one rarely noticed because she was afflicted with an enormous goiter that was a large brown collar, not unlike the big white collars painted by Flemish Renaissance painters.

As much as she tormented mom, she was great to me. Of course I was the one who went to Wide's Liquor store to get her Gordon's Gin, which she drank straight, no ice, no water, no tonic, absolutely straight. I always knew when she called me with her "bank" in her hand that I was off to the liquor store. Her "bank" was a great blue polka-dot handkerchief in which she knotted large bills in one corner, one-dollar bills in another corner, and various denominations of coins in the other corners. Her bank was stored between her ample breasts. When I returned with the gin, she was generally already rocking in her rocking chair on the front porch with clouds of smoke gently circling around her. I knew that I could sit on the top step and listen to the rhythmic rocking and the wonderful stories about who we were and where we came from. I truly loved her. She always told my father I was the one that told the truth and that if anyone could be counted on, it was Junior, who was me. I can only once remember her hurting my feelings.

We were nine people and two bedrooms. Dad and Mom had one bedroom, which left one for seven people when Gramm was home from her live-in job in Dover, New Jersey. I had to sleep with her. One cold morning when I was seven or eight, I awoke to feel a foot in the small of my back. Startled, I suddenly became airborne instants later, with a stinging pain as my naked butt bounced off the cold wooden floor. I remember bursting out of the bedroom to tell mom that Gramm had kicked me out of bed. When mom saw me standing there with a perfectly perpendicular woody, she became hilarious. Between her bouts of uncontrollable laughter, she said I could never again sleep with Gramm and from now on would have to sleep on the couch in the living room. Years later I understood.

Being consigned to the couch in the living room meant I would be taking up space my mom needed to run her washing and ironing business. I slept in the living room of our next house, too. She kept the light on most of the night, working mostly on shirts that I delivered in the morning and in the afternoon after school, once I started going to school. I learned not to sleep a lot. I kept mom company and learned much about the post slavery days in the South and how her priority was for all her children to be educated. During the day, mom cleaned houses all over that town and later Englewood and beyond in Bergen County. I'd do my homework after delivering shirts, which was a problem, because my sister Alice was the apple of my father's eye and she got A's, and my father and my teachers sang the same song: why can't you be like your sister Alice? But when I stayed up with mom and delivered shirts and finally began to clean house with her, I felt better about myself despite dad, though my grades were never as good as Alice's.

We had moved to that small, two-family house in Englewood two years earlier. I was born in Morristown Memorial Hospital in Morristown, New Jersey in 1931. At that time, the family lived on a small truck farm with crabapple orchards in nearby Booton. My father cared for the orchards and did other landscaping chores for the owner, who also owned the houses and land. My father's cousin Sam and my mother's twin brother Eddie all worked together on the orchards as well as doing landscaping jobs. We lived in shanty row houses all connected together, clapboard painted gray with green roofs and shutters. In front of each house was a three-step stoop. In the summertime the stoops were a great meeting place. Our houses were so small that the three families could sit on their stoops talking, joking, laughing, singing, and enjoying each other without raising their voices. The ladies were great. There was mom, Sweet Gal, her brother's wife Josephine and her sister Sara and Sam's wife Urla. Sara's husband had passed away from galloping consumption, and she had a touch of it. Whenever she coughed up blood, she went to the sanitarium for several months and came back. Josephine washed her dishes, utensils and other pans in separate dish water. No one was allowed to drink or eat from anything after she had used it. No one got sick.

The houses were situated on top of a small hill overlooking fields that were used for growing hay. Between the houses and the fields there were row upon row of clothes lines. The ladies, except for Gramm, who had that live-in housekeeping job in nearby Dover, ran a laundry service: sheets, pillowcases, shirts, underclothes and all the rest. These things were washed on metal washboards in huge galvanized metal tubs with brown bar soap and bleach. The whites got bleached further in the sun, and all the clothes had an amazing fresh smell to them. Urla, Sara, Josie and my mom were the Coppertone ladies of the stoops. The stoops and the front yards were their domains. When the laundry, the outside laundry, the housework, the outside housekeeping, the cooking, and the caring of husbands was finished, they sought refuge in untethered conversation with each other.

The women seemed to be everywhere, ever vigilant over the eight children. At that time we were a few months to four years old. We roamed unchained and unrestricted about the fields. Then suddenly one of the ladies would swoop down, grab you by the scruff of the neck, and flick you out of trouble or danger. If a young one gave a hunger cry, its mother would snatch him up, bare a breast and nourish the child. She kept working, ironing, dusting, folding clothes as she did so. Saturday evening, the daily chores done, everyone had to take a bath, a weekly ritual. Fathers first; then they were off to card games. New water was drawn from the only faucet—cold water heated on the stove—and then the youngest came first and the same water was then used to wash us all with that same laundry soap. There was no running hot water, so the water got heated on our pot-bellied wood- and coal-burning front room stove. That pot-bellied stove was a staple of the all-purpose room that served as the kitchen, dining and living room. In the end, whatever water was left was taken to a nearby creek and discarded. We were then rubbed down with Vaseline. At last it was time for the ladies to bathe and to do each other's hair. This was an elaborate undertaking. Soon as one had bathed, the hot curling irons that had been heating on the stove were brought out and the hair-straightening, curling and braiding began. The stoops turned into a beauty shop. The women's wonderfully attuned bodies were a product of the hard work they endured. Their flexible, lithe movements, their positioning on the stoops in their clinging, soft cotton, brightly colored dresses, their Peter Pan collars that opened down the front—it was like watching ballet. So too were the holding the head back to wash their hair, the attitude of their heads between their wide-spread knees, and the maneuvers the hair-dressers had to assume to keep from burning flesh as they straightened hair. Saturday night was a beehive of activity and murmurs punctuated occasionally by an "ouch" and a stench of burned skin as one of the performers misplaced the curling iron and touched a scalp or neck.

That pot-bellied stove was infamous to me, because Reggie, my cousin, who referred to himself as "Lucky Falcone," ran me into the red-hot stove, which caused a quarter-inch indentation in my forehead. No one had money for a doctor, so a chip of ice from the ice block in the ice box was wrapped in a dish towel and held to my head until the bleeding stopped. That indentation plays an important role in the makeup of my forehead today.

Some ten yards or so to the right of the front of the house was a large double-seater outhouse with newspaper for toilet paper. It tended to be an extremely cold place in winter.

Each time mom had a baby, her brother Eddie and Josie had one. When each had four children, my dad looked around at our common bedroom with its plank, knotted-pine floor from which some of the knots had fallen out, permitting us to look from the bedroom into the kitchen below. He said we had to find a larger place, which meant getting another job. Dad kept his landscaping job and found a second job with Faber's cement block factory in Paramus, New Jersey. Faber's was owned by two recent immigrant German brothers. One tried desperately to be American and treated his black employees as less than human. The other brother came to our house, played pinochle with us and brought us gifts. Once he came and 'Amos 'n Andy' was on the radio. 'Amos 'n Andy' was a lame radio show predicated on poking degrading fun at Negroes. Mr. Faber made my father turn it off. He said it would make us believe we were truly inferior, and if we listened enough, we would accept the low expectations and estimate of our worth that were depicted.

Finding a place to move a Negro family in the 1930s was fraught with major problems. There were whole towns in New Jersey that would not allow Negroes to live within their borders. So major was the problem for Uncle Eddie, mom's twin brother, that he moved in with his relatives in Philadelphia. This prompted Dad to visit his cousin Janie Scruggs in Englewood, which resulted in our moving in with them. Twenty-eight Armory Street was a two-family house of plain cement block, a first floor with a porch and a second clapboard floor with a closed-in porch. Janie was married to Sam, who was light and damn near white, with one of those pencil-thin Smiling Jack mustaches. He specialized in not working and running after women, especially those with big behinds, the kind of behinds in which the left buttock would say to the right buttock, "If you let me by this time, I'll let you by next time." Janie had such a behind; nonetheless it did not seem to keep Sam home. Besides being big-butted and a bit overweight, Janie really was pretty. She had taut, glowing, beautiful bittersweet chocolate skin and large dark brown eyes swimming in the whitest sclera you ever did see, matched only by her pearly white teeth. When she smiled, lights went on everywhere. Her regular job was cleaning house, but her specialty and most lucrative job was playing Aunt Jemima. Aunt Jemima was the black face on the box of a very popular pancake mix. She dressed the part and served brunch for wealthy families on the knob hill of Englewood and Englewood Cliffs. Sam, her husband, played her like a drum and sniffed out each payday, showing up and taking whatever money she had not hidden. No matter what he did, she forgave him and always took him back. Her generosity extended to our family, too, and she rented us the closed porch, one bedroom, and shared privileges for the kitchen and bathroom. We were then a family of seven.

The two bedrooms were occupied by Janie and Sam in one and Janie's mother Anne Scrubbs in the other. She was wracked with spinal arthritis that kept her permanently bent over so much that her face was parallel to the ground and at a 90% angle to the rest of her body. She had all her faculties, but she was afflicted with a weak bladder, and any time she coughed, sneezed, strained, or lifted anything heavy, she would squirt urine. Her urinary incontinence was so bad she was rarely without the stench of urine. Anne Scrubbs was a legend. She wore several pairs of bloomers when she started her rounds in the morning, and by the time she returned her bloomers were soaking wet and the urine was dripping into her socks. Before I started kindergarten, I went with her on her rounds. She had one of those old, railroad, iron-wheeled baggage carts. She started out on Armory Street and ended at Dr. Stapleton's grocery store on Dean Street, about two miles from home. Dr. Stapleton, a white man, owned our house. He lived on our street and owned four or five houses. Annie, on her way to Dr. Stapleton's, picked through garbage all the way up Palisades Avenue. Palisades Avenue was our main thoroughfare and contained some thirty or more stores, restaurants, bowling alleys, and movie theaters. She stopped behind the A & P Franklin Grocery, the Elite Deli, and the Woolworth Five and Ten Cent Store. Finally, she'd pull that rickety old iron-wheeled wagon clickity-clackity over the railroad and trolley tracks to Mr. Stapleton's grocery. She would take all the fruit and vegetables that Dr. Stapleton's clerk felt were too far gone to sell. On the way back she'd pick up the stale day-old bread from the two bakeries. What she didn't eat or get us to eat, she gave to the Scott boys, who kept animals. Living there in those crammed quarters and learning to share the one bathroom was harder than living with that two-seater outhouse in Booton. Ma Scruggs also collected rags and cardboard boxes that she flattened, tied in bundles and sold to the junk man. She did the same with glass and pieces of old iron. Whenever her daughter, Auntie Jane, had her boyfriend living with them, Ma Scruggs was confined to her room, and the rest of the house was a battlefield between Jane and her man. As soon as the money was gone and the boyfriend disappeared, Auntie Jane took her frustrations out on her mother, who was one third her size. She beat her and then locked her in her room or out in the hall. One day the wailing and shouting were particularly loud. We found out that Ma Scrubbs had died in the night. Months later, when her daughter Auntie Jane got around to cleaning the room, she found that Ma Scrubbs had left $11,000 stashed away in old boxes. Auntie Jane moved away and bought a house on Humphrey Street, and that friend of hers, Mr. Bill, moved in "permanently."

Englewood was a city. Its lifestyle was totally different from running around out little truck farm and playing with our cousins every day. Englewood had a population of some 13,000 nestled in the northern Hudson Valley three miles from NYC and the George Washington Bridge. It was widely known as the bedroom to New York's Wall Street community. Palisades Avenue was a beautiful elm-lined street that ran north and south and hosted most of the stores. There was a magnificent one-story high monument to the fallen soldiers of the First World War. Bands came from all around on the 4th of July to play, pray, and give thanks for liberty and freedom. There were some stores on Engle Street, Grand Avenue, Dean Street, Van Brunt Street and to a lesser extent on Englewood Avenue. What divided the town east to west was the railroad, which was the major means the Wall Street bankers and businessmen used to reach mid-town NYC. The RR and Grand Street, which became Engle Street northwest of Palisades Avenue, also divided the town into the hill district, which was often dubbed the seven sisters, like the hills off Via Veneto in Imperial Rome. Big mansions and elaborate estates dotted the hill district landscape that was inhabited by white Anglo-Saxon Protestants. People like Gloria Swanson, Bing Crosby, Artie Shaw, the Armour Meat family, captains of industry, bankers, businessmen and NYC hospital physicians and professors. There were absolutely no Negroes living there other than as Negro servants on some white estates. A small middle class lived around Palisades Avenue and to the west and north. The very large slum area was politically termed the 4th Ward, which was becoming at that time increasingly black and known as "Little Texas." Lincoln Elementary and Junior High School served the 4th Ward children. Those schools were essentially black with a student body of 600 or more, of which there may have been as few as three or four white kids.

There were far more whites who lived in the 4th Ward, but these houses were salamandered out, sometimes one house at a time, so that the white children could go to the 3rd Ward's essentially white Engle Street school. When we moved to 28 Armory Street with Janie Scruggs and her family, Armory Street was changing, and white families were moving out. Armory Street is just a one block street left off Palisades Avenue when traveling west, away from the Hudson River and one block from the monument—just one block long but a total microcosm of the country if not of the entire world. My experiences with the people of that block so impacted my life that even today every now and then I simply drive through to remember where I came from and from where and from whom I escaped. I renew my self-esteem, my self-expectation and vow to be of service in this world. I thank God and whatever powers that may be for having given me the courage and perseverance to arrive at this point in my life, where my love, my experience and my skill can truly help. I know I must continue as well to love and broaden my intellect and talent.

Armory Street: A Microcosm of America

On Armory's Street's east corner with Palisades Avenue was the Lightning Auto Store. That place sold electrical supplies as well as auto parts, and they were extremely busy. The two- family tan brick house next to the store was owned by a white widow who rented the second floor to the McCoys, who were black. They had a son named Skeets, and despite becoming a homosexual in high school, he became an all-state sprinter on the track team, all-state guard on the basketball team, and running back on the football team. Skeets became infamous in his last year at Dwight Morrow High School. Englewood had a great basketball tradition, having just graduated the great Sherman White. The year after Sherman's graduation, the team had a gifted center named Chris Thomas and a terrific sophomore guard named William Dismus. The team had won the Northern New Jersey High School league and were going to play for the Eastern United States Championship at Glenn Falls, in upstate New York. Skeets was assigned to sleep in twin beds in the same room with Dismus the night before the big game. During the night Dismus awakened to find Skeets trying to mount him. Dismus put up a tremendous fight and succeeded in kicking Skeets off the bed. But in doing so, Dismus smashed through a window, severely damaging his foot. He couldn't play, and Englewood lost the Championship.

The next house was a one-family stucco. Mr. Spivey, a black, lived there with his wife and two daughters, Carolyn and Gwendolyn. Their neighbors were the Pierottis, recently immigrated from Italy. Mr. Pierotti had a tailor shop on Palisades Avenue. He was friendly with my dad, but ours was the only black family that he would allow his two sons, Frank and Peter, to play with. Mr. Pierotti got so furious that a black family moved in where a white one was before, next to his house, that he built a fence up the middle of the driveway to keep the black family from using the common drive. It seemed to me that all the immigrants acted the same way. They treated blacks as inferior. It was as if they got a card, when they entered the USA, that directed them to treat blacks poorly, never associate with them, and in short never give a nigger a break if you wanted to become a good American.

One morning after church, I was sitting on the curb in front on our house. You need to know that Armory Street was just wide enough for one car to pass, if cars were parked on both sides of the street. The front yards were no deeper than three or six feet with a simple walkway to the porch. Most yards had a bordering hedge, and most of the yards had no driveway at all and only space to pass single file into the tiny backyards. Now on that Sunday, Carolyn and Gwendolyn were playing with a ball. Somehow the ball bounced over the illegal fence into the Pierotti's yard. Mr. Pierotti, his brother, their wives, and Peter and Frank were sitting on the porch. Mr. Pierotti grabbed the ball and told Carolyn he was keeping it. Carolyn ran into her house, and Mr. Spivey came out and asked for the ball back. The Pierottis said the girls were making too much noise, and he was keeping the ball because it came onto their property. Mr. Spivey worked every day for Allied Moving Van Lines. He was chiseled. He dropped off his porch in just his pajama bottoms, flip-flops and ribbed sleeveless undershirt. He wore a silk lady's stocking on his congolene-plastered hair. I sensed there would be a fight, but before I could call my dad to help, Mr. Spivey had shuffled up onto them Pierotti's porch stairs. Once he was on the porch, the Pierotti women retreated behind the screen door and the men and children jumped up to stop Mr. Spivey as he went for that ball. Mr. Spivey shook them off like a large Newfoundland dog would shake off water. The boys went flying. The men were pummeling him until with one mighty crack to each of them, Mr. Spivey knocked them stone cold, flat on their backs. I realized then that my dad was standing behind me and asking why I was calling him. Mr. Spivey was so quick, my dad had seen nothing but the police coming. When I told my dad what had happened, he said, "Boy, Mr. Spivey don't need no help." The police department ordered the Pierottis to take down the fence.

There was a driveway on the other side of the Pierottis, shared with another black family with which Mr. Pierotti had no trouble. That was a single-family house run by Mrs. Bishop and her mother Queenie. I went to school with Mrs. Bishop's daughter Margaret, who was an absolute tomboy. She beat us at sports, and when she felt like it, she beat our butts. Mrs. Bishop's husband, Margaret's father, was in jail serving a 25-year sentence because he found his girlfriend with another guy, and he shot him dead. He should have been released on good behavior, except that each time he came up for parole, Mrs. Bishop would come before the board and get him committed year after year. He was agonizingly serving every minute she could get him.

Queenie, Mrs. Bishop's mother, was another problem. She was a severe asthmatic, and at times you could hear her wheezing from across the street. Worse than that, she was a fixture on the front porch of her house, and as soon as my dad came home, he checked in with Queenie. There was no reprieve from her reports on me or my siblings' activities during the day. Dad accepted her version as to what went on as absolute gospel. A bad report from Queenie sent you on a trip for dad's rod of correction, which was a covered electrical cord. There was no such idea as child abuse then. Our father would not let us play kick the can and other street games, and there were only two or three families whose children he would allow us to play with. If he ever caught us with them, we'd get a spanking. My father couldn't stand the street we lived on; he couldn't stand the people. His attitude toward grades was the same. If you didn't get As or Bs on your report card, you got a real strong talking to the first time, and the second time you got whooped.

Mrs. Bishop's neighbor to the south was Dr. Willoughby, who lived in a red-brick single-family house. Dr. Willoughby was a general practitioner who sutured up my scrapes and lacerations several times. He was a Negro doctor, an absolutely cookie-cutter type of the doctors being produced by the two Negro medical schools, Fisk and Howard Universities. That is to say, he was light-skinned to nearly white with good near-Caucasian hair and Caucasian features. He had a small office downstairs and living quarters upstairs. Decades later his grandson went into the NBA straight from Englewood High School along with Moses Malone and Daryl Dawkins. Next to Dr. Willoughby were the Gordons, who were in service to wealthy white people on the hill. She was a maid and cook, and he was the chauffeur. He was always immaculately attired with his quintessential cap, form-fitting jacket, and black knee-high polished boots shined to a mirror sheen. He drove down either the classic black Lincoln Continental with the whitewall tires on the back or the convertible tan Packard Roadster with chrome trimmed running boards with really broad band white wall tires tucked into special pockets alongside the engine just behind the two front fenders. When the top was down on that one, there was a second windshield between the driver and the passengers. No other car excited me as much, ever. Everyone came out to look at it each time he brought it home. The Gordons were good light-skinned Negroes who treated everyone with respect and gave great goodies at Halloween. They had no children.

The next single-family brick house belonged to the Pierces. Their daughter married an American Indian and moved to Virginia, where they had three children. She sent her first born, Earl, back to live with her mother. Aside from his reddish Polynesian-type skin, he looked Caucasian, as did his brother Reggie and his sister Joyce, who came up for summer vacations. Joyce was my first love and my first date. I hunted for soda bottles and turned them in so I could get money to take her to the Saturday movie at the Englewood Theater. At that time, Negroes could sit only in the balcony. I bought two tickets, but we shared one seat. I had enough money to buy a box of Cracker Jacks that contained a ring that I promptly put on her finger, and we became boyfriend and girlfriend. I'd like to say our relationship lasted a summer, but it was probably more like a week. I was about eight. As years passed, Joyce came back more beautiful than ever, with flowing, naturally straight hair. She didn't know I existed. I was clothed in my blackness and also, though I didn't realize it, my poverty. The Pierces had porch parties to which my kind—really black people—were not invited. Only light-skinned people could come. Mr. Pierce worked at the Post Office. Being black and working for the U.S. Government was equivalent to being an astronaut today.

Earl's later history was remarkable. He ran the mile, was a champion pole-vaulter, went to the University of Pennsylvania, became an air force pilot and a jet ace in the Korean War and went on to be the first black general in the USAAF. I remember Earl for another reason related to the colors of our skins. Coach Smith, who was white, was our high school track coach. I ran cross country and threw the disk for him before I started to play basketball. Later, when I got my six-year contract to study medicine in Bologna while playing professional basketball, I went to the school to say goodbye to him. Instead of congratulating me, he said, "Now Earl Brown looked like a doctor. You don't even look like a doctor." That slammed me. It really hurt. I had graduated from college, become an Air Force Officer, and played in the NBA. But my Negroid features were not Earl's Caucasian features. It was the white looking one that should become a doctor, in his mind. I just mumbled "shit happens and then you die" and turned away. I never spoke to Coach Smith again.

Next to the Pierces were the Gilberts. They were also light-skinned Negroes who had one child. After they divorced, their son Jimmy spent the winters at our school and the summers with his father in Harlem. Each year he came back wilder. He cut his hair different, wore pegged pants and Zoot suits with thick gold chains and began to smoke reefers with the older kids on the corner of Englewood Avenue and Humphrey Street. Finally he was in and out of jail. I last saw him from under a grand piano at the Memorial House recreation center. I had raced and dived under that piano when one of Jimmy's NYC pals started fighting and pulled a gun. Some of the locals were wrestling the gun from him. That was because Jimmy had brought a bunch of his New York City boys, all fitted with large brimmed gangster hats, to a dance. When the local girls refused to dance with them, the local boys started to fight Jimmy and his gang. At the first crack of gunfire I dove under that piano. Once our country boys got that gun away, they took delight in beating those city boys and sending them back across the George Washington Bridge.

Dr. Stapleton, who owned the fruit and grocery store, owned the next house on Armory Street. He rented that house to the Grants. Leroy Grant was in my class and was probably the brightest kid in the school when we were ten. At that time, I helped my mother clean Dr. Jenkins' office across the street, a job that decided me on becoming at doctor. Leroy decided the same thing. We collected rags, paper, and bottles for money to buy chemistry sets, stethoscopes, doctor bags, and blood pressure cuffs from the back-page advertisements on Action Comics. We established a lab in Leroy's basement. Working to help mom clean up at the end of office hours, I discovered that Dr. Jenkins did his office surgery at that time, and I could watch in the dark waiting room through the keyholes into his brightly lit surgical suite. I watched him sew up cuts and drop ether through something like a catcher's mask onto cotton, which put the patients to sleep for more important surgery. He even took out tonsils in the office. At that time Negro surgeons were not allowed to operate at Englewood Hospital. Any patient that needed major surgery, a black surgeon had to turn him or her over to a white surgeon. Dr. Jenkins worked so hard and saw such a huge volume of patients that he became rich and moved his practice from Armory Street to Engle Street, which was the class street for white doctors. He purchased a Cadillac and built a house on the hill down the street from Gloria Swanson.

The community reacted. The blacks said, "There goes that nigger riding around on our money," forgetting that he had helped to make them well. "He thinks he is too good for us. Now he has to live on the hill with all the white people." They forgot that the hill was simply a better place to live, and he had earned the right to live there. The whites said, "Look at that uppity nigger trying to be one of us. He is getting out of place." They were overlooking the fact that he had the largest volume of work and was being paid the lowest rate per case. The blacks refused to come to his new office in large numbers, and the whites did not use him in large numbers. His practice collapsed, and he took a full-time job at the Harlem Hospital in their Home Care department.

Leroy and I were considered exceptionally weird dudes. We fixed the broken pigeons, children, guinea pigs, cats, rabbits, dogs and mice of the neighborhood with tape and popsicle sticks. Once, Leroy and I saw a

Dachshund with its stomach dragging the ground. I had saved some partially used cans of ether from cleaning up Dr. Jenkins' office. We picked up the dog. It could scarcely walk. We took it down to the lab, anesthetized it by placing ether-soaked rags over its nostrils, and tied it to the table. Then I took a paring knife and cut down the forelegs to the hind legs through an incision right down the middle. There was almost no bleeding. We pulled back the skin and the muscles and to our astonishment we discovered six little puppies, each in its own fluid-filled transparent sack. We sewed up with ordinary needle and thread. The dog delivered her puppies shortly after that. Years later that dog was run over by a car. After Leroy got out of the service from World War II, he found he couldn't get into medical school in spite of his excellent grades. When I came home for the holidays from Duquesne University in the 50s, I was told that Leroy Grant had been arrested for impersonating a doctor. He had a large, lucrative, but illegal practice.

Big Hutch was the next neighbor. Mr. Hutchinson had a beautiful milk-chocolate, velvety colored girl with flashing eyes and a smile to match. Her name was Joan. She was in my class at school. Smart enough, but if you were not light-skinned you could forget about it. I rarely if ever saw her in that house. It was a huge house, by far the biggest on the street and sort of set back from the others with a large yard and a wide driveway that led to a multi-car garage in an expansive, well-manicured, healthy green lawn that terminated on the banks of the creek. The parties that were held out there were legendary. The cars docked in the front were the best Cadillacs, Buicks, Lincolns, Packards, and LaSalles. Flashily-dressed hard-looking men arrived and left at all hours of the day and night. At night, the men were accompanied by extravagantly-dressed ladies of the night. Black, white, Chinese red, chartreuse and lilac-colored dresses seemed to be the rage. All the dresses had plunging necklines that cut nearly to the navel and made little effort to hide the nipples of their unbridled, bouncy breasts. In summer they wore a mandatory boa; in winter the3y wore furs, mostly fox. Classic spiked-heeled black or white pumps were the shoes of choice. There was always a mighty party going on. In summer you could always hear blues and slow drag music wafting forth from the ever-wide-open windows, and the party lights in the back yard never went off until dawn. Big Hutch was the numbers king. Rumor had it that Big Hutch paid off the police and was responsible for wiping out one competitor down on William Street at the Wides Liquor Store.

Next to Big Hutch was the house of the right Reverend Harris. He was a light-skinned man who lived to be over 100 and was the minister of the black Presbyterian church on Palisades Avenue. Sometime between my

8th and 10th years of age, I was a two-week summer Bible school teacher for him. The reverend was not the point of interest in his house; that was Gladys, his daughter, who was looked like Ava Gardner except for her glowing dark peachy skin that covered a truly voluptuous body. As youngsters we sat on the wall of Memorial House, directly across the street, to watch her. In the summer, she came home at about 5 PM. She had a summer teaching job in New York City. No matter where we were, we'd stop playing and say, "Let's go see Gladys." She never disappointed us. She was like the apple in her preacher father's Garden of Eden. She always waved at us—her boys. We also never missed seeing Big Hutch and his men rubber necking out of the windows to catch her marvelous rear action.

The Memorial House was a social recreation center for the children of the 4th Ward on the corner of Armory and Englewood Avenue. It was a handsome building of dark red brick, dark green shutters, and a green tile roof built in a Spanish hacienda style. A two-story room with skylights was the main open area. Off this room were other rooms where meetings and lessons went on. In the basement there was a large swimming pool that had been converted into a basketball court. The basement also held rooms for boxing clubs, pool, ping-pong, shop and art studios. The building was open 3–5 and 7:30–10 PM every day except Saturday and Sunday. Staffed by white and black social workers and many WASP volunteers from the hill district, the Memorial House activities kept us slum kids off the street and out of trouble.

My father would only let us go to church and the Memorial House, especially me. Since it was the only way to get out of the house at night, I signed up for every course I could from 7:30 to 10 every night. I did art, workshop, open recreation, boxing, cooking, personal hygiene, and drawing. Art was doing murals and working in oil and watercolors. Dr. Alvin Jenkins' wife taught that course. Like her husband, she was light enough to pass for white. She was pretty, well made, with large, soft deer shaped and colored eyes, a natural fair-skinned beauty and prone to blushing. Her voice was so soft and melodious, you thought she was singing when she spoke to you. The workshop was great; we made bookcases, tables, and wooden figures. Open recreation was an hour to play pool, at which I never became any good. I wasn't any good at ping pong, either. I played basketball in that swimming pool that had been dug out further and leveled out. Once, though, I was waiting to play, sitting on a wooden bench with my head against the cement wall, when one of the players crashed into me, driving my head into the wall and knocking me out cold. I was out for who knows how long, and for days I was off balance and seeing double. I never went back to that pit.

Boxing was another story. Between 11 and 15, I never weighed more than 98 pounds, skin and bones with huge hands and extremely long arms. I was called the Spider. No one my age or weight wanted to box me because of my reach. Dickey Standard, a professional boxer who was our coach, had no trouble getting me beat up. He had two guys several years older who outweighed me by 20–30 pounds. One was Patty Best, a white Irish kid with startling jet-black hair and even more startling quick hands, especially his left jab that he used to tattoo my face and keep out of range. The other guy was a black kid who fought in a crouching style. No matter what I did, he seemed to get inside my guard and deliver great hurtful body shots. Whatever way I tucked my chin behind my shoulder, he hooked over and under my jab. Sometimes after those shots he followed up with an upper cut from either hand. Coach Standard made sure I got beat up at least twice a training period. Outside of training I won all my fights. The road work, the light bag, the sparring, the heavy bag, but most of all the jump rope for 15 straight rounds made my legs strong and gave me outstanding stamina.

Cooking class was great because we learned and got to eat what we made. I especially loved the pasta dishes: spaghetti, macaroni and cheese, tomatoes and meat sauces. Dr. Jenkins taught the personal hygiene class, including how to groom, how to blow your nose one nostril at a time, how to cut your nails, how to shower well and dry off, how to nap, and how to dress according to the weather. He would really put you down and embarrass the hell out of you if you showed up dirty or smelly. I went to drama class just to get out of the house. If I finished my homework by 7:30, dad would let me go. One play I remember was a Perry Mason murder trial, and I was a witness who fingered the murderer. But the one I remember most was a comedy that took place in a circus where the owner was trying to get me to go into the lions' cage to feed them. The lions were roaring like crazy, and the owner says to me, "For crying out loud, don't be afraid, those lions were raised on milk, just like you," and stuttering, I replied, "Yeah, but I eat meat now!"

After practice one night, the boys were all vying for the right to walk with Doris Bailey, a light-skinned girl who lived up on the hill in a gatehouse to a large estate where her family worked as domestics. Her home was a mile and a half from the Memorial House. As I walked up to the group, she said, "I want Junior to walk me tonight." Frankly I had not thought about girls since my debacle with Joyce Brown and the Cracker Jack box ring that summer five years before. Doris and I were in the same class, sophomores in high school, so we talked about school, the play, the work she and her family did for the white family, and how she enjoyed living on the hill. Somewhere along the way she took my hand, and we were holding hands starting up the steep part of the hill. It was around eleven o'clock at night, and no lights were on in the big mansion or the gatehouse. She steered me behind the gatehouse, pointed to a window and said, "That's my room." We were behind a 7–8 foot high hedge. She pulled me forward and kissed me gently fully on the lips at first, then harder and sort of licked them open and began exploring my mouth with her tongue. I wasn't sure I liked that, when suddenly I felt a stirring, then a rise in my pants just like I found in my shorts each morning. She must have noticed it too, because she grabbed it and squeezed. I felt my pants being opened. She guided my hands into her panties. I felt the soft, tightly curled hair and the softer mound underneath. Then I felt my fingers slide into a moist, sticky, messy feeling substance just as I was feeling something had gone wrong. I didn't understand what was going on. I felt her rubbing my ear and whispering, "You're so smart. You know just what to do." I was in a daze as she lay down, her panties off and her skirt up to her neck. She pulled me on top of her and introduced my penis to her insides. She started wiggling and moaning, and I held on for dear life. I was holding her tight now, feeling the hardness of her nipples. I became aware of the fluid around my penis getting hotter and hotter, and she pulled me ever tighter to her. She started a loud moan that she finished off by holding her breath for a long time. She held me so tight and began biting me at the same time. I found myself biting my lip, became stiff, sucked in my breath and began to shake all over.

I'm not sure how long we lay there, but she found her panties, dressed, kissed me, and slipped into the house. She said, "I'll see you tomorrow in school." Once under the streetlight I saw that I had sweated through and through, there were grass stains on my pants, and there was a white residue around my zipper. My hands smelled of that sticky stuff. I trotted home. It was after midnight when I saw the light in the living room where mom was ironing. I was feeling strangely wiped out, and felt I really had to sleep. I prayed dad was asleep, and thank God he was. I went down the hall and slipped into the kitchen, completely avoiding the living room and mom. I heard mom say, "Is that you, Junior?" I replied I had to go to the bathroom. There I scrubbed away the sticky substance on my hand, washed the white residue from around my zipper, and tried unsuccessfully to get the grass stains off my pants. It must have taken a long time, because when I came out my mother said, "I thought you fell in." I simply replied, "How you doing?" To which she replied, "I'm doing what I have to do, son, doing what I have to do."

Going west on Englewood Avenue from the Memorial House was the synagogue, Temple Emmanuel. The rabbi came to the house and tapped on my window Friday, Saturday, and Jewish Holy Days. He needed me to turn on the lights in the synagogue. Sydney Lerner was Jewish, and he played with us and had taken me there the first time to turn on the lights. The synagogue had a basketball court where we went often to play. Sydney's father had an Italian food store on Palisades Avenue. My dad said the Jews were the smartest white people because they worked the hardest and spent extra time studying. They also went to their religious school after they finished with our school day and went to school both Saturday and Sunday. And they stood up and spoke in their religious school, which made them more at ease for public speaking and expressing themselves. All that extra studying made ordinary schoolwork easier and kept them asking questions and staying ahead of their classes. My dad said you could not have a better friend than a Jew, so long as you remembered that if you Jewish friend gets into a fight with another Jew, you can't jump in because then there is a 100% chance they will both attack you.

Another Dr. Jenkins, this one a dentist, lived on the west side of the synagogue. He was another light-skinned medical professional, a fine dentist, and extremely busy. He had a white lady hygienist who was reportedly his lover for years. Continuing west on Englewood Avenue was the office of Dr. Nicolson, a light-skinned Negro gynecologist who specialized in abortions. He had a very large in-office illegal abortion practice for both black and white patients. Without a doubt he was the wealthiest person in the 4th Ward. Next to his office was the Black Masonic Temple, to which my dad and my brother David belonged. Two houses further up was Dr. Smith's office. Dr. Smith was very dark, like burnt toast, which was extraordinary for a doctor of color. Alas, Dr. Smith was a Jamaican who held on to his West Indian accent for dear life. Jamaicans were like any other immigrant trying to make sure that no one, white or black, mistook them for an American Negro. Forget about that truly black skin; just hear that accent, man. Two houses up Bennet Road on that corner was the White Elks Club that as the area changed to 90% black became known as the Black Elks Club. My brother David belonged to that, too. Next to the Memorial House, coming full circle, was Mr. Campbell's house. He was Jewish and wore his yarmulke all the time. I never saw his wife. He lived the life of a recluse, making and repairing furniture in his basement. Occasionally he would have a yard sale and suddenly our street would be filled with Orthodox Jews buying everything he made. Though Mr. Campbell's house was originally a one-family brick house, he divided it up so Dr. Alvin Jenkins could have his office downstairs and live in the back of the office. On his photograph, Dr. Jenkins appeared for all the world to be white, but alas in those days a drop of black blood meant you were 100% black, not blended or mixed race. As I explained, mom cleaned his office as well as laundered and ironed all his clothes and lab coats. Watching Dr. Jenkins decided me to become a doctor. Our neighborhood had about all the black professional men in one block: the two Dr. Jenkins, Dr. Willoughby, Dr. Nicolson, and Dr. Smith.

I remember some other houses and people as well. Next to Alvin Jenkins was a house owned by Mr. Banks, an observant Jew who owned a wonderful bakery on Palisades Avenue. His daughter had naturally curly, flowing black hair, eggshell white skin, and large almond-shaped eyes. That family helped stabilize the neighborhood. They gave bread, cookies and cake to everyone. Their neighbor was Mrs. Platt, a beige-colored woman of average beauty but an outstanding body. She lived alone, spent much of her time in church, and took weekly baths every Saturday morning around noon. I know that because she used to come to the porch and yell down that she needed someone to go to the store for supplies, food and a newspaper. If you did her errands, you would climb the stairs to her apartment and get the money so you could go to the A&P on the corner. Invariably when you returned, the door would be unlocked and she would yell, "come in and lock the door." Then she would yell, "put the groceries in the kitchen and come in here and wash my back." When you came into the bathroom, she would be standing, making sure you saw her completely nude. Then she settled back into her sudsy tub. "Could you wash my back?" We all felt she was just eccentric. I used to go there when I was maybe 9 to 11 years old and had not a clue, even though I was one of the boys waiting for her Saturday mornings and would run to get there first when she yelled. I washed her thoroughly and enjoyed peeking over her shoulders and watching the warm sudsy water trickle off her breasts and her rosy nipples.

Downstairs in her house lived Mr. Scott and his two boys, Vance and Billy. Mr. Scott was a music teacher who gave private lessons. The Scotts were light-skinned people. Billy, the oldest, had one blue eye and one hazel eye; otherwise, he was normal. Vance was another kettle of fish. He collected animals and raised some animals, including chickens, mice, rabbits, guinea pigs, and pigeons. He also had lizards, snakes and a couple of cats and dogs. He gave macabre Punch and Judy shows, setting up seats in his back yard and charging admission. Usually he broke something on an animal, a wing, a leg, or a neck. Leroy and I got most of our patients from the Vance Scott shows. Next was a cement block house with a clapboard second floor. Deacon Whittey lived there. He was an extremely light-skinned black man with white man's hair and a bountiful white mustache. He was caretaker of the AME Zion Methodist Church on William Street. My dad was Methodist, and when I was older, my dad rented me out to plow—with a horseless plow—the church's Victory Garden. For a time, dad went to church with mom, but the Reverend Pearson was a Ph.D. in Theology who lectured more than preached with fire and brimstone, and dad said he needed that fire. Dad also thought Reverend Pearson didn't stick close enough to the Bible. My father had gone to third grade; he taught himself to read the Bible and read it to us every Sunday. He became proficient enough in reading and speaking to be the shop steward at the Gibraltar paper mill in North Bergen, New Jersey.

Deacon Whittey had a lovely black wife who was a major league player when it came to church outings in the park. Her table was the first to sell out of the greatest sweet potato pies and coconut cakes. They had a pretty, petite grand-daughter, Geraldine, who had flawless skin and hazel eyes. She was nice to everyone. While she was not as well-endowed as Gladys, the preacher's daughter, she was close. The Andersons lived downstairs from the Whitteys. They were hard working brown folks with three boys much older than I was. The eldest, James, was lighter than his parents; Sam was brown like his parents; Arthur, the youngest, was positively black. James worked; we didn't see much of him. Arthur ran card games in his garage, and he allowed the loft in the garage to be used for, well, other things. Sam, the middle boy, was in love with Geraldine. They had been boyfriend and girlfriend through high school.

One morning in summer, after their high school graduation, I woke Sunday morning to yelling and the sound of running feet in the alley behind our house. Soon the police came and asked if Sam Anderson had come into our basement. "No," I heard mom say. They she asked "Why?" The policeman said that Sam had killed Geraldine and the boy she was with up in New York City—shot them both. The word was that Geraldine had thrown Sam over for a light-skinned, pretty city boy. Sam Anderson served seven years for the two killings. Some of the church ladies said it was all a shame, because the boy Sam shot was damn near white.

Next door to them was a brown clapboard house with yellow trim. It was a real den of iniquity. The Flemings lived on the top floor. Mrs. Fleming was a full-blooded American Indian, and her husband was a light-skinned Negro. All of their children were light-skinned with black Indian hair that their daughters wore in magnificent braids. Marie was the oldest in that family, and she was an unabashed lesbian. Jimmy, the lone boy, was simply average at everything. He got left back twice, which made him bigger than anyone in his class and the classic bully of the school. He used to beat me up on a regular basis when I was small, so I often walked two blocks out of the way, which was difficult, because he lived just two doors down from me. Eventually my sister Alice, who was two years older than me, put up a good fight with him and scratched his face up pretty well. After that he bothered us less. My brother David and I also developed a whistle signal when we got in trouble with him, so he had to fight all the Johnson boys at once.

One winter evening, shortly before Christmas, there was light moist snow falling just at sunset. We were starting supper. All of us were seated at the table when we heard a wrenching scream. The crying out in the street sent chills up my spine. My dad rushed out as we waited at the windows. Dad returned to tell us that Mr. Fleming, who drove a gasoline delivery truck, had slammed on his brakes to avoid a car that had darted in front of him. The sudden braking caused the truck to jackknife. The truck and the gasoline it was carrying burst into flames and Mr. Fleming was burnt to a crisp.

Downstairs from the Flemings lived my friend Chris Thomas, who was known as Fats. The house was rented by his cousins the Craigs, who took care of Chris, because his parents were dead. Fats was two years older than I; he had another cousin, James Craig, who lived two blocks away and was in my class. He came over to see Chris often, and we would play when I wasn't busy doing something with Leroy. At that time we were all between ten and twelve years old. After a while, another cousin, Freddie Craig came to live there after he got a less than honorable discharge during World War II. He was a brown, strange-looking man with a small Caucasian nose but enormously flabby lips. His lower lip hung from his mouth like a miniature balcony. He licked his lower lip constantly, leaving an ashy outer border. As soon as Freddie arrived, he started buying all the local children candies, sodas and ice cream from the Goldberg Candy store across the street from the Lincoln Elementary School. One evening a lot of us kids got together to play hide and seek. Freddie joined in. Once the game started, I raced for the doorway of my cellar. I made it down there, and then Freddie came crashing in after me. We went down the stairs into the coal bin. We could see the kids running around upstairs. When I turned to go back upstairs, Freddie jumped into my space and tried to kiss me on my lips. Horrified, I felt his roughly shaven beard against my face. Some kind of metallic odor exhaled from his nostrils, and his breath was hot and foul. He seemed to have bathed in Aqua Velva. I wriggled free, raced upstairs, and instead of going back outside, I burst into the kitchen to find my dad eating. He said, "Did you finish your homework?" I responded, short of breath, "No." He said, "Guess what." I said nothing more, turned, and went to the dining room and started my homework. I never played another game of hide and seek.

Next to Fats' house lived a grass roots preacher who did love to discuss the Scriptures. Romeo and his wife Juliet were friends of my father, and they lived on the first floor. Romeo was a Holy Roller minister who led a small church in Dumont, New Jersey, where they later moved. Then the Rochesters moved in with their two daughters, who were in their mid-twenties. A parade of guys came through there day and night. Those girls were light-skinned, as were most of the people of color in the neighborhood. The Mears lived upstairs. Mr. Mears was a well-respected carpenter who could build anything, though he drank too much. His wife yelled at him all the time. They had three children, Julie, Leola and Bobby. Julia was in my sister's class, and Leola was in my class. Bobby was two years younger and became too friendly with Freddie Craig, Sissy Sam, Skeets McCoy, Bo Kemp, and Charlie Platt, who were the out-ot-the-closet homosexuals in our little neighborhood. At least once a week Mr. and Mrs. Mears fought over his drinking, and she called him a good for nothing nigger. One Sunday he appeared with a black eye, a swollen lip and a patched nose. He went missing. We found he had answered a call to go work in Alaska where he is reportedly still working 60 years later.

Ours was the next house, and our other neighbors were the Solomons, light-skinned Negroes. They had a son we called Red Fleet because he was red-skinned with kinky red hair. He went around giving shows about the Dozens. His most famous was a show called Signifying Monkey that was absolutely like rap. The Solomon's bedroom was exactly across from our bathroom. There was no air-conditioning in those days, so in summer 12" by 18" screens were placed in the windows. Sitting on my toilet, I could see through their bedroom, through their bathroom, and into the next house. I discovered all this one summer Saturday night. After my Saturday bath, I heard the Solomons talking in their bedroom. I turned out my light and peeked around the edge of the shade. I saw Mrs. Solomon, a roly-poly yellow lady. She was trying to get her husband, who was hiding behind the Amsterdam News, to perform his duties as a man and a husband. She was unsuccessful that night. However, I did check them out four or five times more. I got to see several extremely labor-intensive acts before my mom came in one night to go to the bathroom and found me sitting in the dark. She didn't even move the shade to see what I had been looking at; she simply grabbed me by the neck with one hand and ushered me out into the hall. She dug her knuckles into my temple and whispered, "Do it again and I will, so help me, absolutely wring your neck." I knew what she meant because down on our truck farm I had seen her literally run down and wring our free-range chickens' necks, snapping them expertly. I had visions of those chickens wrung and crazily running around with their heads bouncing around below their necks.

Beyond the Solomons lived a family of recent Italian immigrants, right across from the Pierottis. Mr Sirleppico, a landscaper, lived with his wife Mary, who every now and then sent spaghetti and meatballs down to us.

We sent sweet potato pie and southern fried chicken to them. My dad and Mr. Sirleppico traded tips on growing roses, which they both enjoyed. The Sirleppicos had two daughters, Maria and Grace. The last house before the auto repair shop was owned by a young police officer, George Young and his wife. They were Irish, and he was a motorcycle trooper. He stood six-foot tall and was an absolute showpiece in his uniform. He wore aviator sunglasses, a huge weapon on his hip, and shiny black knee-high boots. He rode an Indian motorcycle that he polished every Sunday. He was a good man who tolerated us kids coming round to ask him endless streams of questions about his job. I never saw him angry or annoyed.

These were the families and children, and the socio-economic environment that exerted a profound influence on my personality.

Moving Downstairs and Going to Work

Several years after we moved in with Janie and Annie Scruggs, Janie, who did so well playing Aunt Jemima, bought a two-family house on Humphry Street and moved out. Mr. Stapleton offered to rent my dad the upstairs so that we could stay there, but the people downstairs, the Nelsons, wanted to move up, so we swapped apartments with them. Their son Anthony was very much overweight, and we called him Donkey. He was nearly six feet tall, as was his mother, and he became a good basketball player with a fine three-point shot. They were both yellow, the "in" color on our street. She was a heavy domestic who did a lot of housework. Mr. Nelson, though, was just about five feet five inches. She beat up on him so often that he was, like Mr. Mears, barely recognizable if he did not have a black eye or raccoon eyes from a broken nose. He worked hard as a janitor, but he loved to gamble, drink and find comfort with other ladies. He always came back home, though, and he always paid physically for his indiscretions.

Since we were seven people living in a porch and a bedroom upstairs, we didn't have enough furniture for the two bedrooms, dining room, living room, kitchen and bathroom downstairs. We accepted whatever furniture the Nelsons left behind, and we all came down to clean up our new apartment. We started in the kitchen, where we found a badly chipped enamel-topped rectangular table with a utensil drawer and four chairs placed around it. We were all standing close to the table when mom casually pulled open that utensil drawer. To a person, our eyes bulged out as if we had all suddenly come down with Graves disease, and collectively as one we jumped up and back ten feet. The drawer was literally filled with cockroaches. Layer upon layer, too numerous to count, every size, every shape, and so packed in that when they started to fly and jump their wings rubbed together making a sound like a typewriter. Their colors varied from every type of gold to tans,

27

browns and blacks. In those first fractions of seconds, their totality obliter-
ated the bottom of the drawer and this dazzling array of colors was like a
Byzantine tapestry in Ravenna, Italy. All of us but mom were shocked into
catatonic statues. Mom's nanosecond reflexes had her dumping the drawer
contents onto the floor, and from nowhere a broom appeared in her hands
and she was killing roaches. The roaches were dead, dying, fleeing into the
different corners of the room and into cracks around the radiator pipes,
light fixtures and window sills. I was suddenly jolted from my stunned state
to realize the roaches had all but disappeared before I could lift a hand. We
stood there in shamed silence as we had done little to help mom. As she
flipped over the drawer, a few stragglers were left for us to kill.

Examining the now empty drawer we saw shell carcasses from dead
roaches, their fine sand-like droppings, and broken limbs. The drawer was
stained, mosaic-fashion, from all the years of droppings being tattooed into
the wood. Mom was not screaming. She was talking in rapid machine gun
fashion. You would have thought we were all called Junior, because all she
said was, "Junior do this, Junior do that" over and over. Then I felt her push
me, and I understood what she was saying, which was to take everything in
the house to the back yard and burn it up. I corralled my brothers David and
Alexander and we took everything, the books, the mattresses, the rugs, the
icebox, the shades, the curtains, the magazines, paper, and even the toilet
paper and the roll it was on and burned them. Then we cleared the basement, after which we systematically disinfected each room, the living room
first. We all lived there for days, just sleeping on the floor. Day by day we
plugged every hole and every crack after first soaking everything with Raid
spray and putting roach powder into every crevice. Then the walls, ceilings
and floors were scrubbed down with bleach. We washed the windows with
vinegar and newspaper. We didn't use the kitchen for days. I don't remember how many times she would disappear into the kitchen with a mop, pail,
rags and bleach. Then she sprayed enough Raid to create a smog. Of course
she did the same with the bathroom and the living room. I remember having a hard time going into the bathroom because of all the chemical smells,
Room by room, at her insistence and guidance, we cleaned up that house.
Then she painted each room three times. I'll never forget her proclaiming
that we will keep this place so clean that the roaches will go upstairs or next
door—anyplace but here. To make that happen there were no dirty dishes
and no leftover food or bread outside the new icebox. Garbage went out
after every meal, and there was never garbage overnight in the house. On
those extremely rare occasions when a roach appeared in the nine years
we lived there, that would be a signal for mom to reinforce her doctrine of
cleanliness. When dad later bought our house on 226 Englewood Avenue,

not ONE single roach made the trip over some eleven years later. What I remember about that house was that it had three bedrooms, and we fixed up the attic. It was a two-story house, wood frame, with nice pine trees out front and a hedge around the whole yard that was about a third of an acre. We loved it immediately because we were for once in a house by ourselves, and we were on a street where you couldn't hear the people in the next house talking about you, except that the people in the next-door house were the Taylors, who at first would not speak to us because we had moved up from the ghetto, or the slum area as it was known in those days. They themselves were black, but because we came from a laboring family and we had not been born to the Englewood area, we were ostracized. Their kids had a lot of trouble with education. Before you knew it, though, they were talking to us. Mrs. Taylor and my mother were helping one another. Yet the first impulse had been not to talk to this new black family from lower Englewood, from "Little Texas."

Over twenty years later, as an intern at the Morrisania City Hospital in the South Bronx, I was called on to treat an ever-increasing number of bronchial asthma patients. I began to question my patients about their living conditions. I was questioning the widely held theory that bronchial asthma was mostly, if not purely, psychosomatic. I found one common denominator in my patients: cockroach infested apartments. That brought to my mind that cockroach laden drawer, and I could virtually see the dust-like, mite-sized roach droppings and the stains they made on the wood of that drawer. I am convinced today as I was forty years ago that these droppings can be inhaled and stain the bronchial and alveolar breathing tree, causing an irritant force that creates asthma in better than 90% of the cases in the Bronx and may well create something far worse such as cancer of the lung.

Mom made things work. She made jams and jellies; she canned vegetables and fruits; she bought mayonnaise and peanut butter in jars that could be used for glasses later. Potted meat, spam, and hamburger meat were big around my house. Fried corn instead of corn on the cob. Meals of Karo syrup, hot cornbread and butter several times a week. Dad helped out by growing what was called a Victory Garden in the swamp land behind the house. This was our own private land fill which Dad had me enlarge by carrying out the ashes from our coal burning furnace. He added top soil from the second job he was working. That soil was great for collard greens that sometimes grew until mid-November. Those made an excellent meal with fat back and hot buttered corn bread. We used to share the pot liquid. Dad was tight with a dollar. He always took Bermuda onion sandwiches to work, with carrots, radishes and tomatoes. He only drank what he could make, and that was plum brandy, peach brandy, apricot brandy, and grape wine.

Dad was never drunk. He was a right Baptist type person, and if you did the wrong thing he was right up side your head.

I never knew I was poor until I was thirty years old and in my clinical year of medical school in Geneva, Switzerland. An Israeli-born American student named David Bernbaum was discussing wealth with a bunch of us American students. He turned to me and said, "You probably grew up poor and never knew anyone with great wealth." I said, "This is the first I heard of being poor. I have never felt poor. I needed you to tell me I was poor. I grew up right in family love with caring parents." I thought, this is just like driving behind a slow driver. I can't drive his car. I can't spend someone else's money. Worrying about someone else's money would be stealing time from my life. Healthy time on Earth is the most precious wealth we have. I have not felt poor one day of my life.

The summer after we moved downstairs I didn't have a job immediately. I was wandering around the neighborhood wondering where everyone was, when I found them in the Anderson garage playing cards with older guys and talking sex. Not knowing much about cards or sex, I sat listening in silence, sure that someone would chase me away. Someone mentioned baseball and needing gloves to play. I piped up that my dad managed and played for a semi-pro team and had a bag with at least fifteen gloves, hats and balls at our house. Everybody got up in a hurry and scurried over to our porch to be the first to get the glove they wanted. We traipsed into McKay Park. There weren't enough guys, so we sent for players from Jay and William Streets and then all of us from Armory Street challenged the guys from Jay and William Streets. The team that was in the field used the gloves—the gloves were left on the field. When the team at bat had to play, they simply used the same gloves. Who knows who won. When we tired of playing baseball we went further into the park to play on the dirt basketball court. After hours of playing we picked up the bag of gloves, balls and bats. That Sunday after church, daddy wanted to play catch with his kids. It wasn't a request but a command. My dad was a first baseman on the semi-pro team, but when he played catch with us he became Bob Feller, the pitcher, with a high, hard fast ball. He was obviously trying to toughen us up. David appeared to be his favorite. David was four years younger than I, and he stuck right in there. It seemed nothing was too hard for him.

David eventually got a scholarship to Youngstown University of Ohio for track and football, though growing up he also boxed and played 3rd base. He was called Dynamite. However our brother Alex was our best athlete. He made little moves and skillfully pulled the glove back in the direction of the throw, lessening the sting of my father's hard throws. Alex got an athletic scholarship to the University of Connecticut for track and basketball. Me,

I would purposely miss a few stingers in a row, which would annoy dad to the point that he would say "forget it," because I would spend so much time running after the ball.

On this particular Sunday, my dad couldn't find his favorite glove in the bag. Two others were missing as well. He asked what happened. I said Alex and I had gone to McKay Park to play baseball against Jay and William Streets and that we had used the gloves. "First," dad yelled, "who gave you permission to go into McKay Park? Who said you could use the team gloves? I told you never to play with those guys. They are too old." Finally, he ended his tirade saying "You and Alex find those gloves and get them back. Never touch them again, and you can't leave this yard for a month."

"Come on," I said to Alex, "We have to go to everybody and get those gloves back."

He said, "I'm not going anywhere. You volunteered the gloves, now go get them."

"Daddy said we have to get them together." So I started pulling him. He punched me right in the face. I put a hand under his chin and on his posterior neck under his ear and lifted him off the ground. His feet were walking on air and he was yelling like a coyote. I had to be ten years old when this happened. I was the smallest kid in my class in height and weight. My dad was six feet one inch and about 250–260 pounds, and when we later worked the corrugated paper mill together, he was called the MAN because he could put 500-pound rolls of paper on the corrugating machine all by himself. Simultaneously, I heard the door open and felt myself smashing into the floor. I felt the right side of my face, ear and temple being smashed, and my father's now high-pitched voice hissing out the words, "Oh NO you didn't. Oh NO you DON'T. You ain't fighting your brother. You ain't pulling no SAM in this house." Dad's half-brother Sam had killed his own brother.

With that initial blow, I had dropped Alex like a hot potato. He went sprawling back into the kitchen. Dad followed up on me, punishing me with mighty right and left slaps. He ping-ponged me off another wall. When I ricocheted airborne like a badminton shuttlecock, he delivered a teeth rattling blow that sent me flying into my own piss and partially under the table. With each blow he said, "I can't have no faggots in this house; I ain't having no punks in this house. I ain't having no sissy in this house." He couldn't get me out, so he started kicking me in the back, and my piss turned to blood. Mom came in from church just then. She was always going to church activities. She grabbed a pair of scissors, jumped on daddy the way you ride a horse and began stabbing him in the shoulder, the top of his head, and his back. "You ain't killing my son, fool. You don't have no bad children, and he may be your best child." I don't remember crying. I don't remember my daddy bleeding. I remember scrambling from under the table to stop mom. Dad never laid a hand on her then or ever. I kept saying, "Mom, please don't kill him. When I grow up I'll kill the son of a bitch." The police came, and they talked to mom and dad. Dad never ever said he was sorry, but Mom never hit him again and dad never beat any of us children again. Gloves? The gloves were never mentioned again until right now, as I am writing this.

That Monday, I went early to Memorial House with the intention of asking Fats what dad meant by faggot, punks and sissies. Fats had seen the police at my house. He asked what had happened and I told him. He volunteered, "Your father is afraid you'll become one of those things."

"What does that mean?"

Fats, who was 13, simply said, "They all mean the same thing. If you hang around with people like Freddie, Skeets and Sissy Sam, they will do things to you that will make you weak and turn you into a girl." He told me to stay away from my own house when Freddie was there and never go to the Anderson's garage where they played cards. "If somebody calls you a name or touches you, you kick their ass or die trying. Don't take no shit from nobody, no body."

About that time I was working for Doctor Jenkins and Mr. Rodgers. I got Mr. Rodgers the Daily Mirror every morning and the Doc the New York Times. I also washed the doctor's Buick. For this he paid me 15 cents a week. What Mr. Rodgers did not know was that every penny I made I turned over to Dad, with which he bought savings stamps that he turned in for War Bonds. I turned over all the money I made from the age of nine until at nineteen I got a basketball scholarship to Duquesne University in Pittsburgh. Dad kept all this money and gave back what he thought I needed. Mr. Rodgers was paying me every two weeks—thirty cents. One week he says, "Take this big coin, it's a quarter; it's the same as three little dimes." I presented the same story to Dad. He went to see Mr. Rodgers, came back with a nickel, and told me I didn't have a job. Of course my father found me another job and protested my spending all my spare time looking through microscopes and getting new chemistry sets instead of going to the movies like normal boys. But he even took us, my brothers and I, to some old Negro league games and even once to the Polo Grounds.

The job he found was shining shoes for the Sicilian Brothers Repair shoe shop on Friday after school and all day Saturday, for tips only. I was able to make three or four dollars a week. The shop was just beyond the RR track and Palisades Avenue. Alongside the shop was a bowling alley, behind which were three houses where Irish people lived. The Quirks and the Bests were families with many children around my age, ten to eleven, and we played ball when I had no customers or shoes to shine. The other house belonged to Mrs. Carol, an Irish widow who lived in the St. Cecilia Church. She made me soda bread. Once she took me to the stations around Easter time. She brought me sacred medals, the rosary, a cross, and even one of those bubble-covered statues that simulated snowing when you turned it upside down. She explained that the Little Flower was saintly, and she prayed for snow in August and it came. Everything she had was blessed by the priest. All of them, the Quirks, the Bests and Ma Carol tried to feed me. They Quirks fed me hot dogs and beans. The Bests had lamb stew, and Mrs. Carol had scones and jam. No matter what I ate, I remained prone to awful bouts of hay fever that caused my eyes to run and then cake over with brown-yellow unimaginable gunk. In the mornings me eyes were sealed closed with the thick stuff. Suddenly my nose would start running and then clog up. I'd have violent bouts of coughing that would produce hockers of brown-grey material that I spat out and that then bounced around like rubber tires. Sometimes I would have a sore throat, lose my voice, and have difficulty breathing. There was no money for doctors, even though mom worked for Dr. Jenkins. He charged full fees every second visit. Mom treated me with Vicks Vaporub. I had to swallow some Vicks on a tablespoon of sugar made wet with turpentine. Then the Vicks was rubbed on my forehead and chest, and a towel was placed over my head, which was pushed over a steaming towel covered with Vicks. Several nights of that made me seasonably well.

Mrs. Carol was deeply concerned that one of the Sicilian brothers was abusive to me. As a recent immigrant, he was trying to fit in, so he shouted at me, "Nigger, get your black ass in here. You got shoes to shine." She thought he felt more American when he did that solely because that was the way all white Americans treated all Negroes. Mrs. Carol's struggle with Mr. Siciliano was due to his mean-spiritedness or his not realizing that he was free to treat me as another human being. One day she said his voice, heavy with accent, told her that he was a bad person. Having made this decision, she got word to my dad about my treatment. My dad was looking for an excuse to get me another job because working Friday and Saturday gave me too much free time, even though he had found me more odd jobs washing windows, cleaning houses, painting, plowing, cutting grass, cutting hedges, shoveling water out of cellars, cleaning attics and more. Despite all this I was fighting anyone who looked at me cross-eyed, trying to prove to my dad that I was not soft.

Trying to bolster my tough-guy image, I joined Jimmy Fleming, who was four years older, and Jimmy Gilbert, who was a year or so younger, in breaking into the Lightning Auto Store on the corner around Christmas time. We stole Christmas tree lights. We were so bright that we sold them on the same street, and one of our honest neighbors turned us in as well they should have. Jimmy Fleming had a long record and was sentenced to some juvenile time. Jimmy Gilbert and I were let go because it was our first offense, but we had to show up at Lincoln School with our parents. I was in the fifth grade, and our principal was Mr. Ted Davis, whom everyone called Tex. Mr. Davis was a prejudiced man, and in 1946 when Jackie Robinson was the first Negro to sign a major league contract—Branch Rickey signed him to one of the AAA teams in Montreal—Mr. Davis called all of our school to a special assembly where he announced that Jackie Robinson would be killed and that we should be prepared to forgive and not be too sad, because no Negro would ever play in the major leagues. Mr. Davis told my parents that I was a good student, though not as good as my sister Alice. He said I was polite and respectful, but that recently I had started fighting everyone I could without any discernible reason. "Mind you, he doesn't seem to be a bully. It doesn't matter what size the boy. If something goes wrong, he settles it by throwing punches hot and heavy. And now he's involved in a robbery. What can I make of it? What would you have me do?" He asked my parents who sat in mummified silence, answering only by shaking their heads in a negative way.

We all sat in silence for several moments. I volunteered nothing. Finally, Mr. Davis said, "Junior is a good boy. I refuse to believe otherwise. His grades so far have not suffered. I'm going to make him a junior policeman." My parents shuffled in their seats. He went on in this way: "He'll stop trouble instead of creating it. As a junior police officer, he will be given a shoulder and waist strap with a badge and yellow slicker poncho for when it rains. He'll be assigned to Officer Pat Murphy, who runs our crossing lane and discipline around school. For his duties he'll get a free pass to the Plaza Theater for all day Saturday." Now my dad was amused and beaming. Mr. Davis added, "If that works out, he gets the job next year in 6th grade. If he does a super job, he can cut my grass at home on Ivy Lane and ask everyone else on the block and perhaps cut theirs." Mom was also beaming. She already cleaned house for Mr. Davis and his family, the Alexanders, Rodgers, and Diamonds, all on Ivy Lane. That was a wonderful solution that brought an end to my criminal career. So when Mrs. Carol's report came to my dad about my treatment at the hands of Nicolos Siciliano, he got me another job at John the Hatter's on Van Brunt Street. For dad it was perfect, and John made it perfect for me. I had to get to the store by 7am every day but Sundays, clean out the store and the sidewalk in front of the store, put out the garbage, and fill up the hat washing machine that was used to dry clean the felt hats. Felt hats were the rage. Everyone who was anyone had one, ladies and men. I restocked the windows and showcases with what was sold by way of hatbands, feathers, medals, bow ties and matching handkerchief sets, different kinds of powders used to dust hats, all kinds of felt stain removers and so on. Once all this was done, I had to be in school by 8:45. School was out at 3:05, and I was back in the shop by 3:15 to sew in sweat bands and outside ribbons, place feathers or medals on hats, dust them, and box them in large hatboxes and tag them with tickets in such a way that you could see and read them from the floor. They were often stacked ten feet high.

The owner was Mr. John Paglioni, a first-generation Italian-American. He was a gentleman with a kind face and beaming, happy eyes. He had a perfectly round belly that preceded him wherever he went. It really did shake like the proverbial bowl full of jello every time he laughed, which was often. He sang Italian songs and whistled while he worked. It seemed he was forever telling his wife jokes that made her laugh this rippling, incredibly infectious laughter. Gosh she was pretty. She was for all the world a twin of the movie star Pier Angeli, who as an Italian beauty who had earned worldwide acclaim in the 50s.

Mary took great care of me. She brought me wonderfully crusted Italian bread with butter, special honey with the comb still in it, and hot chocolate for me each morning. I worked at her elbow all afternoon from 3:15 to 6:30, when the shop closed. Whenever she heard me sniffle or heard me sneeze, the next morning she would show up with a real wax beehive honeycomb chew and make me chew it all day. My respiratory problems all disappeared. You could see and palpate the love between them, and I loved them both. I was paid $1.50 a week. But if he had special jobs and I worked Sunday, he would pay me $5.00 that week. I loved them so I would have worked for nothing. They had no children. Mary was always buying me things and giving me things from the shop. I remember one tie and pocket handkerchief set of gold and a sharp real Stetson felt hat of chocolate brown with an even darker brown band, and sticking in it a small Community Chest red feather. The guys teased me about it, but not in a vicious way. They were all envious.

In my free time, I continued to send for chemistry sets, microscopes, magnifying glasses, science books—nothing had flagged my interest in medicine. I was still going to be a doctor. One Spring we prepared over 70 hats for the Bergen County American Legion members and their marching band. These were wide brim white, grey and tan hats with chin straps and ribbon hat bands. They had to be cleaned, pressed, blocked Australian style with one side turned up, powdered, and fitted with new ribbon bands. The day of the parade, the hats were ready, and we were proud of the work we had done. We were up most of the weekend completing this job. I had accepted so much praise for the work I had done. Imagine! My work was praiseworthy! For my part, I was grateful to be of service and appreciated. Several hours before the hats were to be picked up, I was sweeping the shop. The hats were nestled on the ten foot high mobile rack. I was using a large push broom. Somehow it got hooked between two shelves and pulled them both down. The white hats tumbled every which way into the pile of dirt that was accumulating on the floor. I heard a gasp from the sewing machine area, which I knew to be Mary. I looked up to see John the Hatter with both eyes clamped shut, his hands clamped tightly over his ears, his nares flared, his lips pursed tight, and his face getting redder and redder. I thought he was about to burst. He wore a dark blue apron that draped down from his square shoulders over his protruding round belly like a tent, and that apron was quivering. My heart sank into my shoes, and I stepped on my heart as I uttered not a word but turned and left the store. I never went back.

Twenty-two years later, I was an intern at Englewood Hospital. I was summoned to the E.R. Someone was about to code. I raced down to emergency, where I immediately recognized John the Hatter. He still had that perfectly round protruding belly, and he was unconscious and in serious trouble. He was foaming at the mouth, and you could hear the rattling from his mighty labored breathing. I pried open his mouth with a laryngoscope, saw his vocal cords and inserted a #9 Shulty endotracheal tube and attached it to five liters of oxygen a minute, securing the airway. The ECG showed a rapid tachycardia, and with the stethoscope I heard rales throughout both lung fields up to his shoulders. I gave him 4 mg of Lasix, 4 mg of morphine, and 0.5 mg of Dioxin IV. The IVs ran at a keep open vein rate. I put tourniquets on three of his four limbs and rotated them every fifteen minutes. After half an hour he had gotten no worse, but there was no perceivable improvement, so I took a hemoglobin and hematocrit reading that showed a normal 14 and 43. I took off two units of blood—a Swiss medical trick that immediately reduced the amount of blood his heart had to push around, and that decreased the work of his heart. In short order he was awake. He didn't recognize me, but he was totally with it. When I spoke to Mary, she knew me even though I had grown seven inches and gained over 100 pounds. She said she'd know that smile and eyes anywhere. I explained what John had: no infarct but heart failure and that he would survive. She embraced me in such a grateful, unreserved loving hug, squeezing me hard at first, then letting her tiny body collapse against me, shuddering with large heaves as she cried a great cry of relief.

Over the next week or so, whenever I visited them in his hospital room, I told them how I loved them and how it broke my heart when I pulled down the hats and saw so many of them lying dirty on the floor. Especially knowing how hard we had worked to make them spectacular.

They explained that they tried to call me back, but I just kept running. They thought I would come back, but I never did. I shared with them how I had become a professional basketball player and then a doctor. As always, they made me feel special. Well 22 years earlier I had fled their store fearing I couldn't undo the trouble I had caused. I went home that day and told my folks what I had done. No one said anything, one way or another.

Several weeks passed until my dad found me another job. He was paying his gas and electric bill at the Public Service office on Engle Street and saw a sign in the Taras Shoe Shop window. The owner needed temporary help to move his shoe shop from there to Palisades Avenue less than a block away. It was the height of the second world war, 1944–1945, and there was a manpower shortage. After seeing how well I helped him move his store, Mr. Taras, who was the owner and shoemaker, decided to keep me on to clean up shop and run errands like getting food for the 10 o'clock coffee break and the lunch hour. Getting food was sometimes a painful experience across the street at Baumgarten's Restaurant. As a black person, I wasn't allowed to sit down or eat there, but I was permitted to order food, stand by the cash register until it was ready, pay, and take it out. Now if you came in and the waiter started taking your order and some white customers came in, you would be unceremoniously dropped until she finished their order. It was that way at the Woolworth five and dime lunch counter and most other lunch counters in Englewood.

That summer I watched the man run the big machines to sand down the heels, tack on the heels and soles, and use the big Landis machine to stich on the soles. I wasn't tall enough to reach the machine-driven finishing sanders and brush polishers. One day, though, I brought along a pair of my mother's wedged shoes, and wearing them I could reach the whirling brushes and sanding wheels. After several weeks of observing me to see that my hands were strong enough, Mr. Taras built a long wooden platform so that I could run the machines. He was a genius at fixing and making shoes. He was also great at making new machinery. He and his brother John had vineyards back in Italy, and as soon as the war was over, John went straight back. No matter what time of day, John seemed to have some of the vineyard in him. Paul's wife Rose ran the cash register and sold shoe products up front. They had two daughters who were kind to us three black boys in the back. Of course two of those "boys" were grown men. I earned $8.00 a week during the summer, working six day a week. After school started, my salary was reduced to $5.00 a week.

That year, ninth grade, I was one of the editors of the Lincoln Junior High School newspaper and yearbook. I was also president of the science club. That yearbook reported that I would become a doctor. There was a photograph of me peering through a microscope. The caption read: "Fletcher will become a doctor and he will take care of us in one of his many offices." At graduation, I received the American Legion Award for outstanding academic achievement, just as my sister Alice had done two years earlier, but of course my grade average was nowhere near hers.

That summer, dad was shooting pool and learned of a job at the Mary Elizabeth Tea Room on Engle Street. I'd work every day except Wednesday at 25 cents an hour. The hours I worked brought me $12 a week. Mr. Taras took my brother Alexander as my replacement, and I began my career as a salad bar man, dish washer, and janitor. One of my jobs was to open the restaurant on Saturday and Sunday mornings and to walk the owner's dog. One Sunday morning the sous chef asked me to take a breakfast tray up to Mrs. Jackson, the owner. She lived above the restaurant. She was a plump, white-haired white lady with rosy cheeks. If she had worn a beard she could have passed for Santa Claus. I found her in bed with her head resting on Julia's head. Julia was the restaurant's white female manager. Entering the room I nearly dropped the tray. I came to an abrupt halt. Julia drew the covers down a little to reveal they were buck naked. I was speechless as she flicked the ash of a cigar in an ashtray on a cluttered bedside table. She said in her low voice, "Just put it down between us." I nodded and said nothing, set it down, and backed out and walked quietly down the stairs. I ran into the kitchen and whispered to the chef, "Julia is upstairs in bed with Mrs. Jackson. They are both naked, and Julia is smoking a cigar." I expected them to be surprised, but instead everybody laughed. When the laughter subsided, I asked, "What's so funny?" A chorus greeted me: "They are a couple of butches." I said, "What's a butch?"

"You don't know what a butch is?" one of them said. "A butch is a dyke."

"So what's a dyke?" I asked.

Then I heard the sous chef say, "He must be some kind of sissy boy if he doesn't know what a butch is."

Sissy boy was a trigger word for me. In a sudden reflex, I dipped my left shoulder and shot a straight right at him, using the muscles in my right side, right leg and right shoulder. That punch must have traveled ten to twelve inches right to the middle of his forehead. He fell as if chopped down by an axe. His butt hit the floor, and his legs flew apart. Resting on his elbows, he said, "Are you crazy? I'll tear you apart." Ernie was at least 20 years older and 30 pounds heavier than me, so I'm sure he thought "this is not happening!" I said to him, "If you call me a sissy boy again, I will flat out kick your ass." The chef said, "Ernie, you going to let that kid talk to you that way?"

Ernie leapt to his feet and lunged toward me. I got off two really nice jabs to the right of his head, opening up a pretty good cut that gushed blood.

I had a little twist to my fist as my jabs contacted flesh—they hurt and they cut. He could not reach me, so he stood back and felt his head. When he saw the blood on his hand, he cursed and rushed me again, this time diving. I sidestepped him to his right and pushed him to the floor with my left hand in the middle of his back. As he tried to get up, I put both my knees in his back and wrapped my right arm around his neck and pulled back. He started making gurgling noises like he was dying, and they pulled me off him. The chef said, "Ernie, you just got your ass stomped. Now we are all going to keep calling him Junior, but you're going to call him Mr. Johnson from now on." Of course he never called me Mr. Johnson, but he never called me sissy boy again, and we became great friends. He taught me how to rub the wooden salad bowl with garlic and place the vinegar on before the oil and how to chop vegetables and to toss the salads. He always got me the really good food—no leftovers when it was time for me to eat, and from then on he washed his own pots and pans.

High School and a False Start

In the tenth grade, I was fifteen. I had started to grow, and nothing fit. I felt like a scarecrow, and everyone continued to call me "The Spider." Going into tenth grade meant leaving Lincoln School, which was 99% black and going to a school that was 95% white. Unfortunately, many very bright black students had such low self-esteem that they did not continue into high school. They couldn't afford to buy the clothes that other students wore; they were embarrassed by the King's English they heard around them; their families needed them to work, and that offered them an excuse. My dream was still to become a doctor. The high school offered different diplomas in those days—commercial, classical, language, general, academic, and scientific. Englewood was considered the best high school in New Jersey both academically and architecturally. Its huge campus had Ivy covered buildings like Princeton. I signed up for the scientific diploma coursework, but my guidance counselor, Mr. Gordon, changed all my courses to woodwork, shop, and mechanical drawing, leading to a general diploma which was not for college or pre-med work. I asked Mr. Gordon why I couldn't take the scientific course. He didn't think that as a Negro I could do the work, and he didn't think my family could afford to send me to medical school. I told my father, who knew I had been dreaming of becoming a doctor, and he stood up for me. He went to the high school dressed in his best Sunday suit, shirt and tie, and made them put me in the scientific diploma college prep courses. Mr. Gordon assured him I would fail and wind up getting no diploma at all. Dad said I deserved a chance. I passed my science class, but the class I liked the most was English literature. The English teacher became my favorite: Miss Sally Winfield from West Virginia. I'm not sure how she felt about black people, because the first few months in her class were miserable. She called on me so often that my classmates all began to say "OH

NO" when she called my name time and again. Our very first encounter was when she called my name, Fletcher Johnson, and asked, "Where did you get that name?" I said, "My father gave it to me. It's his name, too. No first name, just two last names, slave owners' names." That was greeted with a loud silence.

Englewood's Dwight Morrow High School was a public school, yet one of the absolute best in the state. It sat on 20 acres of prime land with multiple fields and an ice pond in the winter. Dick Button the Olympic champion figure skater went to school and later practiced there. John Travolta and Sherman White went there. It was a regional school. Students came from well to do places such as Oradell and Englewood Cliffs. Miss Winfred's persistent questioning taught me how to learn and the all-important principle of being prepared and participating in class. To respond to her questions and then some, I developed the study habit of getting up one hour early to study with a fresh mind all that was difficult for me and to study the things I enjoyed at night before going to bed. No matter how it started, Miss Winfred made of me a better student. It got to the point that when we did a story or a poem and others attempted to explain its meaning, she would practically always wind up by saying, "Let's hear what Junior has to say." She always liked my version. She gave frequent surprise tests. Sitting right in front of me was a model for magazines like Seventeen named Dorsey. She would have photo shots around the school for those magazines. Dwight Morrow had a Princeton college-like tower and great lawns for photography. She was really photogenic, and she missed a lot of school because of photo shoots. She had wispy strawberry blonde hair, and her eyes were a soft tan in a freckled, pale pixie face. She was about 5'4" and 100 to 110 pounds. One day we had a surprise exam—20 questions, I believe. Of course I finished early, and Miss Winfred walked the aisles monitoring the exam. As she passed me and then Dorsey, Dorsey tried to grab my paper, but I grabbed it right back. Miss Winfred continued walking. When she came back around and passed me, Dorsey turned, looked me straight in the eyes and hissed, "Don't you know you ain't nothing but a nigger? Boy, you ain't going to be nothing but a garbage man anyway." She snatched the paper and copied it. When she finished, she flopped it back over her shoulder without ever turning around. She never spoke to me again, which was no different from before, as she had never spoken to me before grabbing my paper to cheat on that exam.

Within a year, I had to give up the Mary Elizabeth Tea Room because dad wanted me to go to church on Sundays. Besides, some school nights I wouldn't get home until after 11 PM because I had to mop up the restaurant when it closed. I went to work for the Casa Manor Restaurant in Teaneck, N.J. They paid me $1.00 an hour but only needed me Friday and

Saturday nights. I was a bus boy and dishwasher. Dad wanted us all to play instruments, so I chose to play the clarinet with my free time. Sports were out of the question because they took too much time from work. Dad was unhappy with Casa Manor because I would come home at one or two in the morning, and I had to walk five miles from Teaneck near Hackensack back to Englewood through a lily-white section that was dangerous at night for a black person. He was afraid the cops would shoot first before asking questions of a black boy in that neighborhood at 2 or 3 in the morning. So he got me a job at Phil's German Bakery. Even though I worked for the night baker, I rarely got home later than 10 PM. The night baker was a lovely Italian girl who was really a patisserie chef. One day she and I were finishing our work when the news came that the war in Europe had ended with our victory. We ran out into the street. People were pouring from the buildings and stores. There was dancing, singing, crying, laughing and shouting—sheer jubilation. Suddenly this pretty white baker kissed me fully on the lips. I turned and ran into the back of the bakery thinking I would surely be lynched.

In the 11th grade it came time to apply to college, and I wanted to go to pre-med. My scientific courses were going well. One spring-like night in September I heard a rap on the front room window. Looking out I saw a white face and I thought it was Mr. Faber, dad's old boss, but it was Dr. Stapleton, the white owner of the house. With him was a man as black as Dr. Smith, which was pretty black. We six children had come to the door to see who this white man could be, and we were taken aback by the black man who was saying from the hall in a very much put-on West Indies accent, "With all these nigger kids I'm sure this house is a wreck." Dr. Stapleton said, "This house gets better each time I see it. Mr. Johnson fixes everything." Dad hadn't heard Mr. Lewis and his West Indies remarks. Mr. Lewis toured our home with his nose seeming out of joint that he could find nothing out of order. When he left, I told dad about Mr. Lewis' remarks. My dad said, "No, he didn't." And we all chimed in, "But he did, dad." Dad said, "We'll never pay him a penny of rent." He turned into his bedroom, and as we watched he pulled down the shades, switched off the ceiling light and also the small bedside lamp. Then he pulled out his long trunk, the one he went to when he bought something for the six of us, especially our Easter outfits. This time he took out a .45 pistol and laid it on the bed. He lifted the top compartment off the trunk and put it on the bed, revealing a huge compartment full of coins and bills. "I am never to hear about this gun or what's in this trunk. You are to tell NO ONE." In a little over a month we left 28 Armory Avenue for 276 Englewood Avenue, a house my father bought. We never spoke to Mr. Lewis, though we saw him many times on Palisades Avenue. Dad spent his money to get out of that house. He told me, "Junior, I know you want to study medicine, but I had to get this man out of our lives, and all my children have to get a college education, so I can't send you to eight years of college.

My dad's plan came true. All six of us got college educations. My sister Alice got her RN from Howard University, her BS from Catholic U., her MS from Maryland and her Ph.D. from Catholic, all on academic scholarships. My brother Alexander got his BS in business at Connecticut University and an MBA from Farleigh Dickinson. He played basketball and was recruited to run track. The GI bill assisted him financially in obtaining his degrees. David got his BA in education from Youngstown University and his masters from Fordham on track and football scholarships. Ruth Ellen got an associate degree from Toledo, two masters from Temple and a Doctorate in Business from Temple. Robert got a football scholarship to University of Idaho and earned a Masters in physical education from Purdue. He was Olympic track coach in Sydney, Australia 2000. So my dad was right, except that each of us made sure he did not have to pay for our educations.

Years later I came to understand more fully the black Mr. Lewises of the world and why my dad refused to rent from him and bought our own house with his savings. I viewed that decision as a good thing because it was the impetus for us to all to go out and get our own educations. No opportunities like these exist in the whole world. Only the United States affords its citizens and even its illegals great levels of public education. Mr. Lewis was only one of many people of color I have encountered who were born in another country, be it the West Indies, China, Japan, or Africa, who do not want to be mistreated as Americans of African descent. You have to imagine a person of color coming from another country or continent peering through a window, closely observing how Americans comport themselves, because after all they want to be good citizens who blend in and then excel at taking advantage of the abundant opportunities in our great country. What this window reveals are the endless privileges that white skin confers. Quickly the newcomer realizes that while he cannot become white, he can behave in a manner that lets the white man know that he is not African American and therefore should not be treated like an African American. The newcomer also recognizes that the whites view African Americans as dehumanized and that the whites have a loss of conscience that enables them to live comfortably with wanton disregard for what they do to black people. Putting down blacks in front of whites is what Mr. Lewis did that day. Black as he was, he was calling us black and disassociating himself from the slave history of African Americans. The first thing the West Indian, African, Haitian and others does is to hold on to his accent for dear life so that white men hear that difference in accent. Tragically, the effort that these newcomers expend differentiating themselves from African Americans sometimes takes away from the work they need to do to succeed in America. Moreover, African Americans often hear those accents as put downs, which they often are. My dad considered Mr. Lewis worse than a white man putting us down, because Mr. Lewis was a black putting down other blacks. In our case, that pushed my dad to spend his savings on a house rather than on our college educations.

When this happened, I had just been selected as one of the two boys in the eleventh grade to go to New Jersey Boy's State, a program for academically successful students who got to spend a week on the campus of Rutgers University in New Brunswick. As I had never been on a college campus before, it was a wonderful experience. I learned about politics and how the state, county, and national governments ran. You had to run for office; I won my race in the first week of June when school closed. If you were elected, you were invited to Trenton, the state capitol, for a three day weekend, and you got to meet the people who actually held the political jobs and understand how the system worked. I was ecstatic when I returned home. Dad was happy for me, though my exuberance made him sad, because he had to tell me he couldn't afford to send me to college or medical school.

That summer between my junior and senior years I had grown to 5'11" and still weighed less than 94 pounds. I took a job with the Pepsi Cola company starting at 7 AM and ending at 5 PM, six days a week. The job was unloading freight cars of cases of Pepsi and their sparkling water. I threw them onto great stacks in a huge warehouse. Then I loaded them onto Pepsi trucks that delivered them to chain stores, grocery stores, and country clubs. I delivered cases of soda and sparkling water to back doors, cellars, and kitchens where I couldn't go in the front door or sit down to eat. Despite all that, it was certainly more fun than throwing full cases of Pepsi up 15 cases high for the entire day in the blistering heat under a tin roof and no air conditioning. I got to ride shotgun when a helper was on vacation or sick. Along with the taste of the first vanilla ice cream in a sugar cone that my grandma bought for me at a county fair in Booton, New Jersey, when I was less than five years old, a second unforgettable taste came when the truck driver and I, dripping with sweat, trooped back into one store and went up to the counter. The driver said clearly, "Two imported Swiss cheese sandwiches, Gulden's brown mustard, on a Kaiser roll." He paid for them and took two Pepsis from the Pepsi machine. We sat in the cab of that hot truck with the windows down, and for the first time, I bit down on the crunchy Kaiser roll. My taste buds searched for the treasure inside, which was the Swiss cheese now coated with the tangy deli-style mustard. Boy, did that ever assuage and excite my taste buds! Each bite was better than the last. I started out with a dry mouth from the road, the sun, and some dehydration from sweating, but this mélange of different tastes was beyond good on that day. It was simply magical. Believe me I have tried that sandwich now for 40 years with variant good attempts, but that first one has never been duplicated.

It was the steaming hot, humid dog days of August. The road spoke to the tires, the sun melted the tar that made splashing and splurring sounds. It was actually a dangerous time to be delivering Pepsi and especially the seltzer water, because the bottles would sometimes explode, shards of glass would fly, and you could get cut up pretty badly. That happened not infrequently to a lot of kids, though somehow never to me. That summer, no matter how hot the day or how heavy the work, when 5 PM came, I raced to McKay park to get in the basketball game. People came from all over to play in those games. The games were legendary. We played from sun up to sun down, which I could only do on Sundays. On weekdays after work, I was right there. The understanding was that you had to put up 25 cents per person to play. If you won, you got to stay on and play again. We used the money to buy a pint of ice cream, which was 25 cents. I never played for a team or anything, because my dad thought being in a school sport was taking away time you could be studying or making money.

Sherman White was the star of those games. He became an All American for Long Island University after he helped win two State Championships and the Northeastern USA titles for Dwight Morrow Englewood High School. Sherman was 6'7" and could penetrate with one of the best first steps in the game of basketball, shoot hook shots with right and left hands, and shoot outside shots from the top of the keyhole and the corners. He rarely lost. The other guys wouldn't let me play on his side because I could outjump him defensively, though offensively no one anywhere could match or stop him. He was called Squirming Sherman because he had so many moves. As good as his scoring moves were, his best moves were faking you on defense. Sherman earned every point he scored. We beat the absolute crap out of each other. That summer I weighed nothing, so he knocked me around pretty good. By the end of summer, I was winning some games. We religiously knocked each other to the ground and bloodied each other. The sounds of us thumping each other on the chest with vicious elbows drew oohs and aahs from the large crowds.

One afternoon Sherman and I were sitting talking, eating our everloving ice cream after a Sunday of warring on the court. I told him what my father had said about not being able to send me to premed and medical school for a total of eight years. Sherm said, go out for basketball in high school. You play well enough to make the team and get a college scholarship, and that will take care of the first four years. I told him that I played only on weekends and after work, and that my dad wasn't letting me play sports in school.

When school started, I had to give up the Pepsi job because it was full time. So I got a job at a kosher deli run by Ben Sussman and his brothers and their wives. They had booths and tables that could handle thirty or so customers. They had a very busy counter service for takeout. I became the dishwasher, janitor, and some sort of cook, which included rendering fat from the pastrami and corned beef we made in the basement. The fat cut off the meat was allowed to stew down. We took the greasy residue and made our French fries in them. There has never been such a great tasting French fry—forget McDonald's. I treated pickles in large barrels with dill and spices until Ben proclaimed them kosher pickles. I stuffed sausage and helped the wives make chopped liver, knishes, potato salad, and cole slaw. I was stock boy for all the canned goods. The Dr. Brown soda, cream soda and celery tonic were big sellers. I used to go to the Bronx with Ben to get our supply of kosher meats, bologna and salami. Hebrew National was his favorite. Seeing the rabbi say their prayers and slaughter those huge animals sent a shudder down my back. Ben was always pleasant. He sang "Take the Highway to the Sky" and "Brother, Can you spare a Dime?" and he was great at mimicking Eddie Cantor, the wide-eyed black-faced Jewish man who used to sing "Mammy, Mammy." Black-faced minstrels waving their white-gloved hands were widespread in those days, as was the Amos 'n Andy Show and the Jack Benny Show with his lazy, good for nothing servant Rochester, who was a step-n-fetch-it, slow-stepping, slower thinking character depicting someone who was too ignorant to want more in his life with no desire to work for the American dream, no expectations that he would improve his lot, too ignorant to think he could be educated or be successful, and too lazy to try to improve himself. There were hundreds of examples around to ingrain in the black man the idea that these hideous stereotypes were true and to foster, indeed to embed the idea: "Why try? I can't make it."

Mr. Sussman didn't bother me with his songs. I liked them when he sang them, and I knew him to be a fair, kind and lovable man. I remember once I was cleaning the meat slicing machine and put my hand behind the blade to clean out some debris. Although the machine was off, the blade was razor sharp and damn near took off my right index finger. It was cut to the bone on the radial side. It was gushing blood, but Ben reacted quickly. Wrapping up the finger, he rushed me to the Englewood Hospital where I got five or six stitches. Ben waited and took me home and spoke to my dad. I went back to work the next day, stayed out of the water for a week, and was as good as new. Later, when my dad said I couldn't go out for basketball because I had to work, Ben spoke to him again.

Sussman's kosher delicatessen was closed for the night. I had placed the last of the cole slaw, potato salad, corned beef, salami, pastrami, chopped liver, turkey, knishes, and roast beef into the walk-in refrigerator, where shelves of sturgeon, lox and whitefish lined the walls. There were barrels of kosher dills and containers of sour cream, pickled herring and borscht beets. The showcases were clean; the wood platform behind the counter had been lifted and scrubbed. The floor beneath the platform and the rest of the store was mopped after that cursed slicing machine had been cleaned, and the deep fryer fat had been strained, and it too placed in the refrigerator. The refrigerator soda case was replenished. I left Mr. Sussman to lock up and went home.

Shortly afterwards there was a knock on our door. My father had a puzzled look on his face when he saw Mr. Sussman standing there. Mr. Sussman, a white man, at his door at night in the middle of a black slum. Mr. Sussman walked past my father. Turning, he said, "Your boy is a great help to us. Do you know he wants to play basketball?" Without waiting for an answer, he added, "He should play. If he makes the team he can work after practice and weekends. When the season starts, he can be off those days and receive the same pay. OK, Mr. Johnson?" My dad sheepishly nodded OK. Ushering Mr. Sussman out the door, my father turned to me and said, "What'd you do that for?"

"Wasn't me, Pop. It was Mr. Sussman."

I was not great, but I made the starting team fine because I could put my elbow on the rim at 6'1", and my hands were 11 ½ inches from thumb to fifth finger. No one scored on me, and I got a ton of rebounds, though I was erratic. I would score 15–18 points, then zero to 2–3 points. In fact, we were such an up and down team, we played lowly Clifford Park. The game was in a small gym with a balcony circling the whole floor. It was essentially an Italian team, and they had a band blasting through the whole game: the drums, the drums, the drums. There were cheerleaders and students screaming things down at you the whole game. I scored nothing. We were so bad at the beginning of the season that our coach Tom Morgan felt we would be so embarrassing that he did not sign us up for the annual state tournament. Tom Morgan was a white Welshman and a Villanova star who became a great coach. You definitely could not play for him if you were not attending school and passing your courses. He spoke constantly to your teachers, and if you were sick he called or came to see your parents, and if you were faking it you were off the team. He would come down unannounced to Memorial House and the pool hall, and if you were not doing well at school or absent, he would pull you out of there. He was the football, basketball, and baseball coach, and to be one of his boys meant you didn't smoke, drink, or dress sloppy. He treated his black and white boys the same. Mr. Morgan was one of my patients in later years.

At the games he was an absolute terror. Not so much on the bench: there he was real cool, wearing a pin-striped shirt, pinch collar with a gold pin, neat small knotted tie and brilliantly shined shoes. But once he hit the locker room all hell broke loose. Oranges would fly and occasionally one would land up-side my head. Here in short order you learned the facts of life. To give all you had, to achieve by contributing the part you did best to make the whole outstanding.

We came back with a squeaker against Teaneck. We were tied with them for league lead. Going from the team bus to the gym, we walked a gauntlet. I was popped with pebbles, and some students yelled, "Here comes the cannibal." It was really satisfying when Jack Onderdonk hit a shot from under our basket the full length of the court into their basket. Nothing but net. The last game of the season was at Hackensack. Beating them, we won the JJNIC basketball championship. The Bergen Record ran a picture of me making a hook shot from the corner. Mr. Sussman had it blown up and put in the window. My dad was so proud, he let my brothers go out for sports. Besides my eventful basketball year, the writing under my picture in the yearbook said, "The smile that makes us happy." In another section I was standing with a white girl, and there the caption was "Best Natured." In the sports section I was shown palming a basketball in each hand.

Well, prom time was approaching, and I had no girlfriend. I worked most of the time, and dad was not about to give us money to socialize. But Reverend Taylor, of the AME Zion Church, had a beautiful daughter. I was plowing the church fields for him, so I decided to ask his daughter if she would go to the prom with me. Of course, not being too swift about these things, I asked her on the porch in front of her wise-assed brothers. One of them heard me and said, "Hell no, your black ass is not getting into these high-yellow drawers." There were three or four of them, and they were three to four years older than I. They kept poking fun at my having the nerve to ask their sister, seeing how black I was. I was coming to a real slow burn and backing off the porch I was prepared to fight them all. Suddenly, the Reverend appeared at the screen door, coughed a little, and said, "Ellen, he's a good boy and you can go to the prom with him." God bless the Rev. He defused the whole thing.

After the prom, Ellen and I went to a yard party where there was dancing in the yard and basement. Punch, sandwiches, and potato chips were served. It was getting late, but I couldn't find Ellen. I went upstairs to go to the bathroom. At the door to the bathroom I heard noise from behind another closed door. As I listened, I recognized the voice of my friend William, an All State starting guard on my team. William was high yellow and wore one of those pencil-thin Smiling Jack mustaches. Listening more intently to their lovemaking, I discovered he was screwing my date. I took the stairs two at a time, bolted out the door, walked through the party and straight home. Next day, at McKay Park, I walked up to William, picked him up by the head and slammed him to the ground. I said, "Where do you come off screwing my girl?" "Are you crazy, nigger," he said. "Where do you come off thinking she was your girl? 'Cause she went to the prom with you?" He was rubbing his neck and squirming. Everyone was laughing. I said, "It ain't right." Still, we played basketball. I never saw her again, but William Dismus and I became better friends than ever for life.

I graduated with good grades and my scientific diploma. The only basketball scholarship offer I got was from Coach Lou Little at Columbia University, and that was partial. I would have to live at home and travel to NYC each day. I turned it down because they didn't play in Madison Square Garden, and I wanted to play there, and I wanted to play with Sherman White. Sherman arranged for me to have a tryout with Clair Bee and LIC. They had ten scholarships of which two could be black. There were over 400 kids. The tryouts lasted two weeks.

Charts were kept. How tall, how much weight, left handed jump shot, right handed jump shot, right or left handed hook shot, two handed set shot, how far out, one handed set shot, first step speed, dribbling right and left handed, peripheral vision, passing, rebounding, block out and general defense. The first week we had drills and games among ourselves, and every day ten or twenty boys were cut until we were down to twenty who got to spend the next week working out against LIU Varsity, which included Sherman White, Leroy Smith, Eddie Gard, Tommy Murtla, and above all we played for the great Claire Bee, one of the great college coaches of all time. Mr. Bee was braced by superior assistant coaches. There were Buck Freeman, Buck Lai and the Tiger, Picorella. Picorella personified Vince Lombardi's theory that fatigue makes cowards of us all. Fight the fatigue, the tiredness. When you feel tired remember not to become a coward. Don't give in to it. Reach inside and find the reserve and resolve to adjust and keep on doing the right things. That makes you a winner. Picorella would say it is not the size of the dog in the fight but the size of the fight in the dog that makes him a winner. Just being around Picorella there was no way you were going to be a loser. Dog eat dog, he would say. Then he would line you up against some big guy. He'd pull you aside and say, box him out, block him from the basketball, slide between him and the basketball, flat shoot long re-bound, trap him with a spin and block him under the basket. Arching shoot, short rebound, spread your arms and take up space. Keep him behind, and wherever he touches you, that arm or leg turns to steel. You don't push, you don't trip, you don't elbow. Don't hit. Your arms stiffen to steel and hold without bending them forward or backward. He yelled "No cheap shots" when someone did something dirty.

One of the drills for concentration and eye-hand coordination was making fifty consecutive foul shots to be allowed to participate in full court games. You could do it fifty in a row or five series of ten in a row. Any misses and you started from scratch. Slogan cards were posted everywhere. His favorites were perservere, endure, pay the price, pay your dues for greatness, you'll be number one if you feel you're number one. He said if you practice eight hours a day someone can beat you by practicing ten hours a day. He jumped rope three minutes, then rested one minute and repeated fifteen times while over in other corners of the gym he worked on rebound, individual defense, three-man offense, five-man offense. We were to run miles three hours in the morning and three hours in the afternoon, sometimes in the old LIU Pharmacy gym, sometimes at the Hanson or Carlton street YMCAs, all in Brooklyn. To get there I took a bus to NYC and two subway trains to Brooklyn. I was living and sleeping basketball in those days. Even the rattle of the subway cars seemed to be the patter patter of dribbling or the thud of a ball against a backboard or the squeaking of our sneakers as we stopped short and faked and rolled to the basket in the opposite direction.

We were all seventeen to twenty-year olds. Those were times when I played like fluid drive with reckless abandonment and without reservation. We asked of our bodies energy and we got boundless energy. It came up and bubbled from us, and in a game we never ran out of breath, we simply ran out of time.

Each day players were eliminated. I lasted 'til the end, and the report was that I had no left hand, no outside shot, no jump shot, a decent right-handed hook shot, was an excellent rebounder and defender and had one year of basketball experience. Clair Bee said I needed a little time, and that if I came back next year he would have a scholarship for me. At the end of those two weeks, Picorella came to me and said that I would be a great one because I constantly played above the basket on offensive and defensive rebounds, but I needed an outside shot. He said, "If you come back next year, we'll take you." Well the bottom fell out, and it was as if I had gone right down the elevator shaft of the Empire State Building from the very top floor. Sherman's mother made me a strawberry jello and milk. She said, "Junior, you can make it. Don't give up." I walked home from Sherman's house through the black back streets not wanting to meet anyone. At home I shuffled off to bed without eating. No one had to ask what had happened. I slept for what seemed like days. The next year when LIU held its try-outs again, I thought there was no one better than I. I scored, I rebounded, I played defense and I didn't get a scholarship. Instead, that year the two black scholarships went to Ray Felix, a 6'11" giant and another player named Ed Warner, both of whom went on to become All Americans.

Sally Winfrey, my English teacher from 10th grade, tried to get my father to let her take me down to West Virginia to work on her chicken farm during the summer. My dad told her he had grown up in the South and his son was not going south. When she heard what had happened to me at the tryouts, she got the other teachers to give their personal money for me to go to any New Jersey state college for a year. In those years, one had to take an entrance exam. The highest scorers could go to Montclair State. My scores were not high enough, so I went to Patterson State Teacher's College in the Fall. I took four buses each way.

I spent that year studying business education and playing basketball all over the East Coast with Sherman White and other pick up teams. When I played with the Patterson State team, if Sherman had no game, he would bring some of his LIU varsity teammates to see me jump and rebound. Once he came and was recognized by one of the girls in the stands. She came over seeking an autograph from Sherman. At that time, Sherman was every-body's All American, averaging 27 points a game. The girl was Doris Parks, a honey-colored Bridget Bardot. She didn't attend Patterson State but was a friend of a student, Ida Freedman, a very needy high-yellow. I was going out with Ida, who was from Orange or Montclair, New Jersey. I remember dating her with much trepidation, because she was a light-skinned Negro and all the light-skinned girls in my school were interested in light-skinned boys. Ida pestered me to get tickets for her and Doris to see Sherman play in Madison Square Gardens. Sherman got the tickets, played a great game before 20,000 people, and took us all to a nightclub called Birdland. Ida Freedman threw a party after one of my games and invited Sherman. Sherm had a car, so we went to her place in East Orange. It was one of those parties like the Pierce's used to have across the street and from which I was habitu-ally excluded. Believe me, I should have been excluded that night as well. Sherman and I were the only black people there. They were all mulattos. Ida's boyfriend was there; he was Stan the sailor and nearly as white as his uniform. Ida passed me off to Wynona Nichols, whose skin was so fair you could see the veins underneath her skin. She had a faint resemblance to Faye Dunaway. She was a straight A student interested in bio-chemistry, but for me her personality was Icelandic. Soon the drinks got to everyone except me, 'cause I didn't drink. I could see the guys were getting sick of our sports celebrity. Someone had been telling a joke about how jet-black Nat 'King" Cole was and how his wife was almost white. The joke was that in the middle of the night she would roll over and, seeing a man so black and ugly in her bed, she would shake him and demand, "Nat, for God's sake, sing." Moreover, there was a sheet being passed around to everyone but Sherman and me. Everyone got a big laugh from it. Finally, I snatched it. Someone had gotten some crayons and drawn two big black apes with huge red lips and gaping nostrils. Under one was written Fletch and under the other Sherm. I simply tore it up. I never showed it to Sherman, because then we would have had to clean house with those yellow creeps.

Yellow colored folks' treatment of their darker brethren was the worst of all the atrocities of the enslavement period. Far worse than being thrown overboard from a slave ship because food was short for the white crew, far worse than being lynched for looking at a white woman, far worse than having an eye put out because you learned to read and were teaching others to read the Bible, which was totally against the law of educating slaves, far worse than having a hand chopped off for stealing, far worse than never being able to marry or prevent your children being sold to slave owners hundreds of miles away never to be seen again, far worse than seeing your wife raped by the slave owner, and on and on and on. Far worse because it was and is a visceral and soul deep cry of the black man's desperation to try to obtain the perceived and real skin privileges afforded the white man. However, in so doing, he reveals his self-hatred and low self-esteem and ingrains in himself a sense of being inferior. Nearer my God to thee, and my God be white. Realizing that one drop of black blood makes one black, the time honored practice was for black people not to marry anyone darker than themselves and certainly no one fully black. That credo has stood for centuries and persists as a strong colored thread in the fabric of black life in America.

Another thing that stamped that night forever in my mind was the return trip home. After being stuck in Hackensack three to five miles from Englewood for the umpteenth time, Sherman had muttered something about getting a car. Strangely enough, that night in 1950, Sherman had shown up in a 1936 LaSalle. James, Sherman's brother (famous for having won the 1946 Marble Contest of the entire United States) was driving. James could fix anything, so he dropped us at the party and then dropped another friend Chris at his girl's house. Going back all of us were in that car. Sherman was 6'7," Chris was 6'6," and I was 6'5." We were known as the Three Musketeers. But on that night, we represented too much weight for the rear axle of that fourteen-year-old car. We were making a detour to a strip tease joint called the Club Mombasa, on Route 6 in Teterboro. Crossing a set of railroad tracks, there was a loud snap, followed by a scaping sound and the smell of rubber burning, as the body of the car settled down like a large hen settles down on her nest.

It was so cold out, the windows in the car never defrosted despite five occupants in the car and a heater. The ground was so cold it spoke to you as you walked on it. Winds gusted across the meadowland of New Jersey, chopping our breaths. Freezing to death entered our minds, and as if incorporated in one body we leaped back into the relative warmth of the car. There was an instant silence, born of the desperation of our plight. Sherman ordered his brother to fix the axle in the middle of nowhere, in the wee hours of the morning, in the freezing cold. James simply grunted, "You turkeys are so big you broke the axle. You fix it. I ain't moving. Someone suggested pushing the LaSalle to a gas station and calling someone to tow us in. I imagined my hand frozen fast to the car trying to push it, so I said I would wait with James. Then we started laughing and laughing. Then we tried to throw one another out of the car to go get help. We had wrestled and beat on one another until we were sweating. We finally decided to stop the foolishness because we would freeze before morning if we didn't do something. So out we all tumbled and began running for the Club Mombasa, which was a few miles down the road. Talk about hauling ass, it was one sprint after another until we fell into the Mombasa, and if it had not been for the bar to drape over, we would have fallen to the floor. We were a hilarious sight that night. Three big niggers (as our friends called us) rolling over and over on the bar, panting and sputtering as if we had been running on empty for hours. Our chests were heaving up and down as we sucked up air. Our nostrils and eyebrows were frosty and appeared stark white on our black faces. Tears trickled down from our eyes, and halos of white steam rose from our frozen kinky hair.

Catching our breath and languishing in the warmth with the thought of what we had indeed survived, we finally heard Goldie, the in-house stripper, start to belt out her favorite song, "If I'd a known you was coming I'd a baked a cake." We became hysterical with laughter. Goldie was a fortiesh reddish-yellow Negro lady. She was plump with a chesty endowment and a body which probably through untold abuse and excesses had turned to rolls and rolls of fat. Nonetheless, nightly she dragged her body through a routine of bumps and grinds. She had peroxided her hair, straightened it so that she had these greasy, stiff, quasi-blond braids. On her head she had a gold crown, and she was clad in a "suspect golden 'g' string." By "suspect," I mean I suspected it had never been washed. When we were just about under control, we started laughing all over again, first at Goldie's song and then at ourselves and then at Goldie herself.

Finally, we sobered and I said, "Sherman, I ain't never, no never, coming to these yellow chicks again. In fact, you can take them and shove, man, shove."

Sherman said, "Get off it, as soon as I call, you'll come." I replied, "Don't call me, wait until I call you. Tell you what, Sherm, I am sure God made their society and the area where they all huddle together, the toilet bowl of the earth. So all you need to do is find the chain. Now when you find the chain, then you call me, and I'll flush them out of this world." We laughed until we cried. Later we called John Wright, who owned the Black and White Cab Company, to come get us because we played for his team, the Englewood Flags. He came out between two and three in the morning in his new 1950 DeSoto. As I was leaving the car, the last thing I said to Sherman was, "Find the chain. You hear me, man, I said find the chain."

To skip ahead for a bit, eighteen months later he was on the telephone telling me about a Fourth of July picnic he wanted me to come to because he and his friends were going to play a group of guys from Newark, Orange, and Montclair that included LeRoy Smith, Walter Dukes, Wally Choice, Chucky Gaines, Bub Hurt, and a kid named Fab. I said, "Sounds great, you can count me in." Then he added, "I'm taking Doris, do you want me to bring along Ida or Winona or somebody?" I said, "Sherman, did you find it?" He said, "Find what?" I said, "The chain, man, the chain."

Eight AM on July 4th, 1951, I was sitting on the front porch waiting for Sherman to pick me up. I was feeling low because I had no girl to take to the picnic. Whenever I felt low that summer, I put on my Duquesne University basketball jersey and went out and banged heads in the local basketball game. That jersey accentuated my shoulders, and I liked that. Especially after I had walked up on Red "Fleet" Samuels obviously telling one of his fabled true lies. Red had been in the Second World War in Africa, Italy, France and Germany, and he could tell stories twenty-four hours a day. Most were obviously lies, but he told them with such persistence and sincerity that we had dubbed them "true lies." I didn't know who he was talking about that day when I heard him saying, "That nigger has gotten big enough to whip a bear with a switch. From the back I thought his jacket was packed with 4x4 wooden shoulder pads. They were just that straight. Man, I tell you it's the three meals a day and the meat, above all the meat." Then turning around and seeing I had joined the crowd, he pointed to me and said, "And there's the nigger now." Everybody, including me, started laughing, but it gave me a warm feeling.

Sherman was on time. He was driving a late model Chevrolet. In that Summer of 1951, Sherman White was the most famous person in Englewood and everybody's All American basketball player, and without a doubt the best player in the United States of America. Sherman always seemed to have money. He constantly helped his mother, sister, father and brothers. He was generous to a fault, which caused him to be afflicted with a legion of parasitic friends. I will ever pride myself that then I paid my own way. This attitude Sherman never seemed to understand, but my vibes told me he greatly appreciated it.

I was fortunate to have Sherman White as a friend. He became one of the greatest basketball players in the history of American basketball. On television, radio, newsreels, journals, books and newspapers he was star power personified. Doris Paris was seen everywhere with him. They became engaged to be married, but before that could happen he was thrown in jail for fixing basketball games. Sherman, like all good collegiate players, worked in the nearby Catskills as a bellhop at one of the luxurious hotels and participated in the hotel's basketball team in a very good Borscht League. They made great money and honed their basketball skills during the summers. A lot of gamblers bet on those games and more importantly made contact with the players. Later, in the regular season, the gamblers induced the players to fix the outcomes of their games. This was done by winning games by less than the margin. For example, if a team was a favorite to win by ten points, they would fix the game so that they would win by six. In this manner the gamblers made a fortune by betting that the teams would win by less than the margins.

Sherm, having grown up a good person and in a really good family, at first refused, and the guard that the gamblers had been working with could not control one of the first games because Sherm was such a prolific scorer. One night, after the gamblers had lost a great deal of money because of his uncontrollable scoring, that guard tucked him into a car with some gamblers, who promptly drove him to the end of one of New York's numerous piers, where they threatened his life and the lives of his parents. They also started to bust up his knee and said they would wreck his knee all the way if he did not go along with the scheme. The gamblers, with the team's premiere guard, convinced Sherm that this had been going on for years and that he had better join them.

The way I understand it is that there was a young DA named Hogan who wanted to make a name for himself on the backs of young black and Jewish non-criminal types. Hogan got a law passed that made this point shaving illegal retroactively. Miraculously, Hogan didn't seem to find any problems at St. John's, Manhattan, Fordham, St. Peter, Seton Hall, Duquesne, LaSalle, or Villanova, all Catholic schools whose players also played in Madison Square Garden and in the Catskills. Since Sherman was the biggest star and reportedly had a $50,000 two-year contract with the NY Knicks, Hogan came down hardest on him despite his otherwise totally pristine record. Sherm was sentenced as a felon to a year and a day at Riker's Island prison. He was housed with murderers, thieves, child molesters, embezzlers and robbers. I know of no one who visited him at Riker's Island. When he was released a broken man, Doris honored her commitment to marry him and was viewed by others as a sacrificial lamb and martyr. He accepted a job for an in-house team that featured Sherman, and he played for years in the Eastern Coal Mining league that was stocked with other players whose careers had been ruined by fixing schemes around the country.

Going back to the story, after my year at Patterson State, I went back to try out at LIU for what I thought was a guaranteed scholarship. Clair Bee told me I was ready, but he had only two Negro scholarships and had committed to Ray Felix, a 6'11" giant and to Ed Warner, an inside scorer. Heartbroken, I went home and told my dad to forget about it. I wasn't going to college. By refusing to go to school, I was out of character. My dad picked that up immediately. He did not boot me. Instead he got me a job that would teach me the most important lesson of life, which is that life is short, and if God grants you the chance to find a life's work that you can do, then you should pay the price in time, in effort, in love, and in deferment of pleasures until you have acquired the skills necessary to do that job. Next day my dad had me working with him at the Tomolly and Gibraltar paper mill in North Bergen, New Jersey. During work that first day my dad was laying down the law as to how I was to comport myself. I had all but closed my ears to what he was saying and conjured up images of him kicking me in the back because we had lost his baseball gloves, and I was choking my brother Alexander. I could feel the wet urine with its pissy smell. I heard the hurt when he, beating me, explained that his cousin Sam had killed his own brother and it was not going to happen to his children. I was filling up with anxiety remembering mom riding him like a jockey raining down blows with her scissors, shouting "He's one of your best children." I was once again emerging from under the table tugging at my mom, saying "Please don't kill him. . ..I'll kill him when I grow up." Having my own personal pity party, I barely heard what my dad said, "and furthermore, you, son, ain't going nowhere with the girls down here. Buddy, you ain't knocking one lady up." I was startled by his comments, but it sure did pique my interest. As we pulled into the parking lot, I could hardly wait to see those ladies.

The paper mill was for making corrugated paper. It was tan brick with a tin roof and a sky light. The building went rambling down the hill ending at the rail track where products were placed on flatcars. It was easily 100–115 degrees in there. The central piece of equipment was the corrugator, which was half a block long. At one end there were gigantic struts that held 500-pound rolls of paper. The superior and inferior rolls splayed out over and under a middle sheet of crimped paper that was passed through sand glue. Then these semi-wet papers were pressed together under extremely hot, highly pressured sheets of steel. The sheets became heavy duty cardboard to be folded and wrapped around refrigerators, stoves and other equipment or appliances. My job was to catch the corrugated paper and pile it on the flatcars to be shipped out. The bits of sand from the glue and the sharp edges of the paper cut deeply into our hands, creating scales and calluses to the point that after several days my hands no longer bled.

Dad was right about the ladies of the mill; they were real temptresses. They had that awesome beauty of Clydesdale horses with their curvaceous haunches, powerful legs, and agile bodies. The combination of the heat and the heavy manual labor caused their wraparound cotton dresses to cling to their breasts like Hooters waitresses in a wet sweater contest. They were up for it and up to it. I watched but never touched.

That summer was the summer from hell. My dad took me to work for our 4PM to Midnight shift. We always arrived a full 30 minutes early six days a week. To be late was a cardinal sin for dad; it was both trifling and disrespectful. He signed me up for overtime every day. We finished our shift at Midnight and dad would go home. I would work the next shift for eight hours, making it a sixteen-hour day. Dad came back in the morning and took me home, fixed me breakfast, and put me to bed. He'd wake me up in time to go back to work. He would have a lunch box ready for me with oranges, sandwiches and milk. The drive back and forth with my father gave him a chance to tell me about his growing up in the segregated South, and how he had to leave school in the 3rd grad. He spoke glowingly about his passion for education and his desire to get his children educated. Dad rightly saw education, not skin color, as a way to choices and opportunities to living a better life. He said you must respect and love yourself, then you can love others. Don't do things behind closed doors or in the dark that you would not do in the light of day. In the morning when you look into the mirror, you have to be able to say everybody should love me because I have done nothing to hurt or harm anyone, therefore if they have a problem with me, it is their problem, and my prayer has to be "Lord forgive my enemies and protect me from them." At work, my feeling for my dad grew from fear and mistrust, to admiration, to understanding, to respect, to love, and to great shame for thinking that I wanted to beat him up, yea, even kill him.

Dad at work with a sixth-grade education became shop steward and represented the union in negotiating problems with the mill. He was fair and not infrequently recommended unpaid vacations and actual firing of members of the union for tardiness, absenteeism, and drunkenness.

The workers also called him THE MAN because he alone could load the 500-pound spools of paper onto each of the rollers all by himself without help or machine. Working the night shift while my dad slept made him very proud of me. I loved having him tell people how hard and how well I worked. He was especially pleased because the night shift was always asking him to make sure I signed on because I was the only one who could catch all the cardboard the machines could make at their fastest speed. If you produced more than so many miles of cardboard during your eight hours, all the workers would get an extra five cents per hour. That plus the extra pay for working the night shift was a significant amount of money. Most nights I would hear, "Junior, you all right. We going to run full bore tonight; we done already spent that money." That Sunday my friends thought I was on vacation, because I could only play ball Sunday after church and in most cases I slept right through church.

At the end of August, I told Sherman I was ready to go back to school. My dad had proved his point about not going to school and the working life. Sherman said there was a Mr. Haskel Cohen who was looking for players for Duquesne University in Pittsburgh. Mr. Cohen called me and asked me to come to his office on the 63rd floor of the Empire State Building. Although I lived three miles from NYC, I had only been there twice, once with a church outing and once with school to see Macy's windows at Christmas time. Somehow I worked the subways and got to the Empire State Building. Mr. Cohen asked how I had done. When I told him I averaged four points a game, he was singularly and openly unimpressed. "Well, what kinda family?" I told him that I had three brothers and two sisters. I explained that my brother Alexander was as fast as greased lightning and was already an All State guard. Mr. Cohen said, "Well, do you think I should save your scholarship for him?" I said, "No, I need the scholarship now, and he has another year of high school." He said, "I don't know, you only scored four points per game." I quickly added that we won the NNJBL championship and that I spent the year playing with and against Sherman White. I said I could out jump and out rebound him. "Whoa," Haskel said. He motioned to his assistant. "Call Clair Bee and see if you can get Sherman White on the line for me." Now Haskel wrote for Parade Magazine, he was the first public relations man for the NBA, and during World War II, when there had been no Negro news correspondents allowed at the front, Haskel had represented the Pittsburgh Courier, a black newspaper. Since that time, he had worked recruiting players for Duquesne. Sherman called and said my hands were as big as Sweetwater Clifton's of the Globetrotters, that I could rebound with one hand, that I had a 7-footer's wingspan, and that yes, I could out-rebound him. Haskel measured my wingspan and offered me a scholarship. However, he explained, the two Negro scholarships for September had already been given to Jim Tucker of Paris, Kentucky and Sully Walker of Brooklyn, New York. So he couldn't get me to school in September, but he felt he could get me a full scholarship starting in March, which would mean room, board, books, tuition, health care, gym clothes, and sneakers.

Having already been promised a scholarship the year before at LIU, I felt like I had lost again. I was doomed to failure and had no choice. When I went home and told my dad, he could see how heartbroken I was, and I could tell by his body language that he was desperately trying to tell me how sorry he felt for me. Suddenly, clearly not knowing what to do or say, and shifting his weight from one foot to the other, he said, "Junior, I'm proud of you. I know how hard you have been working. I am going to tell Mr. Fanry, the plant manager, about your year in college and your typing and all, and I'm going to make him give you a job in the office." At first, all I could hear was that my dad recognized how hard I had worked, and he was proud of me. Slowly, I saw a vision of me, 6'2," black as night, with really broad shoulders, with my huge hands curled up over a typewriter with my extremely long fingers daintily pecking out a letter. I grabbed my father and squeezed him to me and started laughing. At first he struggled to be free, then slowly his deep laughter rumbled out and we both laughed 'til we cried.

"Imagine me tip-toeing, black as I am, in my white shirt amongst those white women!" We started laughing again. Finally, I said, "Dad, don't worry, you did a good job. I got the message. I'm going to college as quick as I can." That year I tried out at Fordham University and got a partial scholarship. I tried out at Columbia University and got a partial. I tried out for Seton Hall.

Several days later when dad came to pick me up after my double shift, he said Mr. Cohen called last night and I needed to call him at ten o'clock. I could hardly believe my ears when I heard Mr. Cohen say, "I have a full scholarship for you at Duquesne. Sully Walker turned it down because he wanted to be the first Negro to play for St. John's. You'll be the second Negro to play for Duquesne. Charlie Cooper was the first Negro to play for Duquesne, and Red Auerbach just signed him to play for the Boston Celtics, making him the first Negro to play in the NBA." Remembering watching Duquesne beat Sherman White and the vaunted LIU team in Madison Square Garden in a televised game, I said I would surely like to take that scholarship. "OK," Mr. Cohen said, "Be at Penn Station tomorrow at 10 PM. You'll meet two white players on scholarship also. One is Johnny Masworthy, a 6'5" Canadian-born star from the Long Island High School League. The other is Timmy Cashman, a 6'8" star from the NYC Catholic League." I felt my dad hovering around behind me as I put down the phone. I said, "Dad, I'm going to college. I got a full scholarship to Duquesne University in

Pittsburgh, Pennsylvania. I have to be at Penn Station, 34th and 7th Avenue and they already have a ticket for me."

"I'm taking you to that train right now," my father replied. "You need a blue suit. I'm calling to take tomorrow off." Off we went to Hackensack. We usually shopped at Robert Hall's, but this time he took me to Roger's Men's Store on Main Street. I got a fine dark-blue suit. No one had white shirts that would fit my arms, so we settled for one French-cuff white shirt. I turned the French cuffs down and used a safety pin to hold them in place.

Duquesne

Though the year was 1950, my dad had kept his 1936 black Chevrolet shiny clean and running well by treating it like a baby. Still, I was surprised that he was driving into NYC to take me to the train. Dad hated NYC; it was too tricky. New York folks were too slick, and worst of all was the New York City traffic. He said the guy behind you has his hand attached to his horn and fixed to blast the instant he sees green. Dad was telling me what to do from the minute we got out of our driveway. "Watch out for fast women. Watch for men like Sissy Sam. Don't flash no money. Mind your manners. Don't forget to go to church. If you get in jail, tell 'em to throw the key away; don't send for me. Watch the company you keep. No drugs, no smoking, no alcohol." All this crescendo got him ranting and raving when suddenly he was telling me the story of the American eagle. "The eagle," he said, "makes nest on the highest mountain it can find to protect its young. It goes out and finds food and makes those young 'uns strong. When he thinks they are strong enough to fly, he gets them on his wings one by one and flies them up as high as he can, then he swoops from underneath and sees if they can fly. If they can fly, he lets them go. If they can't fly, he swoops below them, catching them on his wings just before they hit the ground, and he flies them back home until they are strong enough. Junior, I want you to pray hard, study hard, and play hard, but should things not work out for you, you got a home. You been raised right. You're the first Johnson to go to college. I know you are going to do good, but you always have a home to come back to." Dad said a lot of things after that, but I can't say that I remember any of that. I was just full of the paper mill, the heat, the dirt, and all the hand wash he had endured for years to take care of his family. I personally had a debt I could never repay.

Indeed, Timmy Cashman had my tickets. Both Timmy and John were tall blondes better built and heavier than I. They looked like great athletes. Of course, I didn't have a clue as to where Pittsburgh was or how long it would take to get there. Timmy and John obviously knew it was an eight-hour train ride. They had prepared lunches for the long trip. I refused their offer of food, which I appreciated. Mostly I faked sleeping because I was listening intently to their friendly but competitive banter about their prowess. Timmy was saying how he averaged 28 points a game, and John said he averaged 26 points a game, but his league was stronger. There I sat in the darkened train thinking, "Holy mackerel, I scored four points a game! My God! I will be sent packing after the first practice." The more they razzed each other, the deeper I sank into the seat fearing the worst. It was a tortuous, sleepless night.

In the morning, Dudey Moore, the head coach, came to greet us and take us to the home of the Duquesne University Basketball Dukes, up on a bluff. His presence, the simple act of coming to meet us freshmen, game me a feeling of importance. It instilled in me the desire to be the best I could be for Coach Moore. Nonetheless, the trip across town revealed the grime, the soot, and the smog-laden environment of this open-hearth steel center. The sun rose and shone through a veil of soot and particulate matter, creating a rayless sun that appeared to be a large red-yellow-orange ball set in a sea of ominous grey. As I was watching the people scurrying about with their collars dotted with soot, as if sprinkled by pepper kernels, I heard Coach Moore ask, "Fletcher, what do you want to study?"

Startled, I answered, "I want to be a doctor."

Coach Moore questioned me again. "You mean you want to be a medical doctor?"

"Yes."

"Pre-med courses carry any number of laboratory courses. If you miss more than three labs, you will be declared ineligible and will lose your scholarship! Fletcher, we play all over the country, which would guarantee you'll miss three labs, therefore you would lose your scholarship."

Try as I might, I could not speak. After an awkward silence, he asked the others what they wanted to study. I never heard what they answered, because I remained in a daze. When we arrived at Duquesne, I thought about Miss Sally Winfrey, my English teacher who had done so much to make me a student, and I signed up to major in Education. Enrolling in secondary education, I thought, I'm never going to be a doctor, and these guys are better basketball players than I am, and before you know it I will be back in the paper mill breaking my back and busting my butt back on the dirt basketball court in McKay Park, suffering the heckling of the guys in the park. Far too many of them had never even bothered to try. I could hear them say, "You could not play well enough and you wanted to be a doctor, eh Doc?"

Duquesne University was run by the Holy Ghost Fathers. They were a teaching order and had missions all over the country and indeed the world, most notably in Africa. The Pittsburgh mission had played an integral part in the Underground Railroad that spirited runaway slaves during slavery and fed slaves post-slavery as they came from the South to the North. Duquesne had a glorious history in basketball. The first black to play for Duquesne was Charlie Cooper. He graduated the year before I came and was the first black person to be drafted into the NBA. Red Auerbach took him for the Boston Celtics. Dudey Moore decided that all of us would play and live together as his hand-picked freshman team. The Fathers agreed, and in the attic above the chapel they made one huge room with ten desks, chairs, and lamps placed along the walls of the room. Five double-decker 7-foot beds were custom made and fitted with mattresses, sheets, pillows and blankets. There were two Irish boys, Timmy Cashman and Jim Corcoran; two Jewish boys, Sidney Dambrat and Marty Schmer; two black boys, myself and Jim Tucker; one German boy, Billy Rigel; one Polish boy, Mike Brichnovski; one Canadian, John Mosworthy; and one Puerto Rican, Domingo Gonzalez. Dudey was right about living together and playing together. It was an ingenious idea. We became a unit. It was no melting pot but more like a tossed salad as Micheal Mack the great composer would say. Nonetheless, he got a few hate letters about his nigger, jew, spick team. But at that time as freshmen, we were not allowed to play on the varsity. It seemed that fact kept the hate mail light. As a strong freshmen unit, we beat the varsity every practice. The battles were so good that most times we had standing room only at practice. This carried over to our game days when our team played its first game. The Duquesne Garden was filled before the first whistle. The place was sold out to see the freshman game.

As a freshman team we were undefeated against all other freshman teams. During the post season we played varsity players from Duke, Pittsburgh, North Carolina, Notre Dame, Ohio State and Westminster—and we beat them all. We lost one final game by one point to Franklin Elks in Franklin, Pennsylvania. Their team was made up of varsity players from Western Pennsylvania. Thirty-two years later I can still see that final play. In the last seconds, the left forward drives on Johnny Nosworthy and scores on a "Hail Mary" shot. The year ended on that note. I was the team's second highest scorer and second highest on rebound. Although a starter, I played a lot fewer minutes than the 6'8" Jim Tucker, the leader in both categories.

I made the starting team as a forward. Jim Tucker, at 6'7," was center. When the team was announced for our first game, I was announced first and thus became the second Negro to play for Duquesne, and Jim was announced and took the floor later, becoming the third. Oh yeah, I made the starting team after spending that whole sleepless night on the train cringing in fear for my basketball life because of that conversation between those two guys from New York. One had scored 28 points and the other 26. Nobody but nobody scored on me except by accident, and no one but no one, no matter their size, got a rebound on me. I wasn't pretty, but I studied about trajectories at warm up and truly believed every rebound belonged to me. It was personal.

The stories of what went on that year in the loft above the chapel are too numerous to recount, but they enriched my life immeasurably. Educationally, I took every course I could, often carrying 18–20 credits a semester. I carried my books everywhere we went. I struggled the first semester but after that settled into the top tenth of my class. I also joined the Army ROTC. At first, socially, the black community welcomed Tucker and me with open arms. We were invited into their homes, churches, clubs and bars. Tucker was a talker and assumed the leadership role, which I accepted until one evening when we went down to the training table for dinner. We were having steak and potatoes. Tucker was ahead of me in line, and the lady put a steak on his tray, and Tucker said, "I'll take two." Well, the lady said "No," to which Tucker replied, "Father Lucy, who heads the cafeteria, said I could get as much to eat as I want. Now I want two steaks now." "Well, Mr. Tucker," she said, "Father Lucy said you could have one at a time, so when you finish that one, come back and I'll be happy to give you another one."

Tucker perked up and said, "If I can't have two now, Johnson here and me, we ain't eating nothing tonight."

The lady said, "Ain't nothing holding you here."

Tucker shoved the tray back, and whirling, he whisked me back through the line and out the door. I was too pissed to speak. All evening I ignored him. As the evening wore on I got angrier and angrier to the point where I stopped speaking. He got the point and stopped trying to speak to me. Next morning, I was first in line. I started with bacon and eggs, went back for ham and eggs, went back for sausage and eggs and home fries, and as I was downing my umpteenth orange juice I snarled at Tucker. "Listen, sucker," I said, "Don't you ever, no, never speak for me. You got that?" It was the beginning of a beautiful, respectful relationship.

I fell in love with Pittsburgh and all its diversity. While the air was foul, everyone scrubbed down their startling white stone steps and washed their windows tirelessly, keeping the city clean starting with their own areas. Beyond that, the people were hard working and honest folks who opened the doors for their ladies; offered them seats on the buses, trolleys, and trains; said "Excuse me" when the bumped into you, said "Good morning" to you; asked how you were, and looked you straight in the eye while they offered a firm handshake and waited earnestly for your reply. Just good people and die-hard fans.

Academically, I floundered like a boat without a rudder, lost in a wonder world of basketball and the first experience of being away from a small town like Englewood. I was lost in the maze of campus life, the rush of people changing classes, the Holy Ghost fathers rushing around in their long black robes, and always feeling that there was never going to be enough time. It took me the first semester to realize I could not survive academically if I did not formulate a plan to get my studying done. Of course, I had taken too many credits, but I refused to give them up because, after all, weren't they free? After falling asleep with a book one night, I realized that trying to study after practicing basketball was like trying to claw one's way out of prison with bare hands. We practiced six out of seven days a week; we had either Saturday or Sunday off but not both. Each practice was three hours long. Three hours of constant running, jumping, shooting and banging into one another. I bit my lips and got up one day an hour earlier to study, and to my amazement, what had seemed hard and unattainable became clear as day and very easy to understand. So each day I got up early, read the things I didn't understand or had trouble understanding, and like 'magic,' my comprehension was nearly 100%. I developed the attitude that if man made it, or wrote about it, I could understand it with a little more effort. The subjects I understood easily or liked, I could handle after practice. My whole study pattern was developing much like riding a bike, a little less shaky each day. There was nothing I could not learn with a little more perseverance.

Socially, it is fair to say I was backward when it came to dating. There were four or five black girls who kept me going to church and invited me to family Sunday dinners. Growing up in a town where the colored population was mostly mulatto, being as black as I was made a real difficult selling point. At Duquesne University I was suddenly popular with all colors. I didn't pay much attention to it, attributing my new attractiveness to my fame from newspapers, magazines, radio, film and television exposure. I never forgot who I was or what I wanted out of life. I admit it made me feel good to have light-skinned girls ask for my autograph and invite me to their parties and homes. I knew that would never happen in Englewood. Being a wall flower, I certainly did not know how to dance. But the rooms were so crowded, I got out on the dance floors anyway, and when I made a mistake or stepped on someone's shoes, I simply said, "that's how we danced back home in Englewood." Before you knew it, I established a style all my own, and of all things, girls wanted to dance with me. Imagine that!

Although I had a full scholarship, this did not include spending money, so I was in poor shape for dating. I had to find a job to provide clothing and extra money. Mom, dad, and my older sister would send five dollars from time to time. In search of a job, Jim Tucker and I went to the Pittsburgh Plate Glass Factory, where we were given a job working with acid. We were to work every Saturday. On the first day we were met there at 7:30 AM and had our jobs explained to us by a black man who appeared older than his likely age. His face, arms, and chest were polka dotted with large, ugly deformed areas where the acid had eaten his skin away, and the resulting scars were de-pigmented. His hands were scarred beyond belief, and his nails had been eaten back to their nail beds. He could scarcely speak understandable English, yet he tried to tell us what a wonderful job this was and how tough you had to be to win the battle with the acid. While he was explaining how to drop the wax-covered glass into the acid so that the designs could be etched in permanently, I snuck a look at Tucker, whose eyes were as big as saucers. Seeing the fear in his face, I almost burst out laughing. At the noon break, Tucker quit. I would have, but that man, that crazy man, had no one to help him lower the objects gently into the acid that afternoon. So, Tucker lasted until noon and I, being dumber or whatever, lasted one day.

I was still without a job until I was asked to start an explorer group for teenagers in a nearby settlement house on Fifth Avenue. It was a wild part of town at the foot of the hill district. The hill district was 99% black ghetto, and the foot of the hill was no man's land. This settlement house was like a neutral zone where underprivileged Poles, Irish and Blacks met in an unsteady peace. My job was strictly volunteer work, but one night the bouncer quit, and I happened to be there. Mary Stapleton, the director, asked me if I would like to have that job. $2.50 an hour, three hours every night, five days a week after practice. "And how!" I replied. Suddenly I was rich. Let me tell you, though. I did not understand that job. As it turned out, this was a meeting place for rival street gangs, and it was quite a job to service all of them separately and keep fighting to a minimum. I became aware of this abruptly one night when I put a little blond-headed kid out for disrupting the meetings. He went home and brought back his older brother and several others. They rapped on the window where Mary and I were talking. It was twenty minutes until we closed. We ignored them as they continued to call me all kinds of nigger and describe what they were going to do to me when I finally did come out.

Clearing her throat, Mary murmured, "I think they are talking to you." Now you must understand that Mary was a beautiful little blond hidden behind horn rimmed eyeglasses, oversized clothes, and an introverted personality, which seemed to be typical of many social workers. I tell you, that was the last thing I wanted to hear from her. I was so hoping she would say that I should call the police, and instead she came up with, "I think they are talking to you." As I did not answer or look up, she said it again. Silently I moved outside. A great throng had gathered, and apparently I was to be the victim. A 6'4" strongly built man jumped me as I came down the three steps. My arms were too long for him, and I wrestled him off easily. I tried to talk to him and at the same time tried to find out if absolutely everyone was against me. There seemed to be three or four mouthy ones telling the guy who jumped me what to do, so I tried to keep my back away from them. The guy was becoming a physical pain as he pulled at my Freshman Numbers sweater. Without much trouble, I tossed him to the ground, but he would not stay there. He got up and wrestled again. This time I jumped on top of him, pinning him with my knees in his chest. I remember telling him I had nothing personal against his brother, but his brother would not be allowed to disrupt the functioning of the settlement house. I told him I was a peacemaker. Letting him up, I said, "You should go home before you get hurt." Turning to go back into the building, to my surprise, the building was dark. Mary had locked up and slipped away. I was finding that unbelievable when I heard this idiot behind me saying, "See, I told you, all niggers are cowards." I started back toward him. He threw his right fist, which I avoided by pulling my head back. Simultaneously, I dipped my left shoulder, which caused him to move to his left away from this left hand fake and smack into a right cross that I threw with all my body weight transferred from the cement itself right up my right leg, as I moved up out of a flat-footed crouch.

Four dreadful sounds leaped into my brain. First was the sharp crack of my hard fist up-side his bony jaw; second was the instantaneous popping sound as his head twisted madly away from his body (I could sense synapses being torn apart). Third was the thump of his totally limp body as it smashed to the ground several feet in front of me, as if some lumber jack had felled him with a grotesque axe. Last was the sickening sound of his head uncontrollably striking the cold concrete a fraction of a second later than his body.

The roaring silence was deafening. I and the crowd edged closer to him. I was sick to my stomach. I felt, surely he must be dead. I watched helplessly, when suddenly I realized he was breathing. A sigh of relief escaped me as I whispered, "OK." I made eye contact with each of the four mouthy ones, but all I heard was one of them saying, "Will someone help me get him out of here?" It was a cold sweat that accompanied me that night on my three mile walk back to the dormitories. I was heavy of heart because I knew that man lived only by the Grace of God, and had he died, I would be going to jail instead of to school.

Summer came fast that year. Freshman year ended with five of the ten freshman basketball players failing out of school. Summer found me in need of a job. Haskel Cohen, who had got me the scholarship, had promised me a job in the mountains at Kutchers. But I waited too long to remind him. It was strange to be without a job for two or three weeks, because I had been working since I was nine. Necessity fueled my anxiety. I got a job in Charlie Hunton's plastic plant on Van Brunt Street. I got the job even though I arrived at the same time as a 40-something black man arrived, and Charlie said. "I have one job, which is running a hot press." Just like that corrugated paper press, this one had three spools, except this time one roll of plastic fed into the machine over a roll of felt on top of another roll of plastic, resulting in diamond-shaped pressings on felt padded material used mostly for car seat covers. Mr. Hunton said, "Whoever can load the machine has a job." The other man tried, but he couldn't get the 200-pound roll on the top spool. I could, so I got the job. Even today I am saddened by the I.Q. that was needed to get that job. The good part was that I worked from 8 AM to 5 PM five days a week, which gave me the opportunity to play basketball until sundown all day Saturday and Sunday.

In one year on the Duquesne training table and playing Division One basketball, I had grown three inches and gained 50 pounds. Now I was 6'5," 220 pounds and playing way above the rim, all that crowned with a large can of whip ass for anyone who played against me. My rule was, don't start anything, and don't fight or hurt people smaller than myself. If someone did something dirty on me or to one of my smaller teammates, I made them pay. Not infrequently, I punched somebody out to emphasize that dirty play was not about to be tolerated.

My friend Sherman, the All American from LIU, had epic battles with me. I won much more frequently from then on. We played until it was too dark to see the passes or the basket. We would all retire after the games to Sherman's house where his mother would feed us jello and milk in her old frame house on the edge of the park and pump us up with ideas of grandeur, saying, "You boys are all going to be famous someday." Sherman was still in love with Doris Paris, the girl I had introduced him to at a Patterson State basketball game the year before. Occasionally, Sherman and Doris would literally take me on a date because I had no one. Sure, my freshman year I found many young, beautiful ladies curious and willing to experiment. We were young and knew only the missionary position standing, on a chair, in a car, on the floor, rarely in bed. They were wonderful sexual liaisons and taught me the singular joy of sex. Who knows. perhaps I was the only naive one. I shall forever be grateful to them for sharing their young lives with me.

On Labor Day, before returning to Duquesne for my sophomore year, Sherm and Doris picked me up to go on a picnic in Patterson. When we came to Route 4 as it passed Forest Avenue, there was a beautiful girl trying to cross the traffic to get an eastbound ride. She kept tripping off the curb, then jumping back. I had Sherm stop the car, and I jumped out. She certainly was pretty up close. She had a round, dark chocolate face with sunflower colored eyes in clear white sclera, a small pinched nose, pearl white teeth, and small alluring lips that formed a quiet smile when I slipped my arm around her waist, which was accented by a lavender princess dress with a Peter Pan collar trimmed in white by a wide elastic band under a set of perky breasts. I half-carried her across the highway. Reaching the other side, I said, "There you go. Are you all right?" She replied in a musical, melodious voice, "Yes, thanks. I'm OK now." "Where are you going?" I asked. "Reverend Adam Clayton Powell's Church at 125th." I was taken aback, but I asked her name. I told her who I was. She said, "I'm Teresa Brooks, and I know who you are. I'm in your brother Alexander's class at the high school, but this year I'm going to NYU to study music." As she climbed on the bus, I asked for her telephone number. She said it was under Richardson on Forest Avenue. "If you really want it, you'll look it up." I stood there a moment looking after the bus.

Sherm was blowing his horn across the highway. I raced across the traffic. Doris was giggling, and Sherm said, "Man are you crazy? What was that about?" I never bothered to answer, yet all day at the picnic, through basketball games, the baseball game, the jokes, the card games, the food, I kept thinking about the damsel in distress. I could hardly wait to get home and ask my brother about Teresa. I waited for him to come home, and as soon as he opened the door, I pounced on him. "Tell me about Teresa Brooks."

"What's with you?" When I simply stared at him, he volunteered, "She is one stuck up individual. She barely speaks to anyone. She calls the police if you touch her or follow her home. She is a total trip. She likes Alan Sklar, a white guy, and Hudson, who lives across the street. He's older than you and light-skinned. Don't think about it, 'cause ain't nothing happening. She's an untouchable. Just promise me you'll remember I told you first." There were ten days left before I had to return to school. I found her number, called, and went over to meet her mother and stepmother. Her mother was just maybe more beautiful than Teresa herself. Mr. Richardson, her stepfather, was a real upstanding solid citizen who worked in the operating rooms at Bellevue Hospital. We were allowed to go to the movies. Theresa, Terry's mother, made the remark. "All you Johnson boys are good, clean boys. Your mother and father did a good job with all of you." Terry was my first mature love, and I had only seen her once before. It was not Joyce Brown, Cracker-Jack box ring, and sharing a seat at the Englewood Theater. This was the real thing, with all the bells and whistles. I saw her several times at her home for meals and family events that Fall.

About that time I got a phone call from Haskel Cohen, who said that one of the bell hops at Kutchers had to leave, and could I fill in for the last six weeks of summer, until after Labor Day. I could not say no, because Haskel had got me that scholarship to Duquesne. Leaving Terry and our budding relationship, I reported to the mountains, where I played basketball and hustled bags, thereby earning much more money. Terry had been accepted to the School of Music at New York University. She was an excellent musician, who as a high school student had given piano lessons, played for a ballet school, and sung for a glee club that appeared on television. We were going steady by that time, and by the end of summer her mother spoke of marriage. I presented Terry with a $150.00 diamond engagement ring.

We wrote each other frequently when I went back to Duquesne. I stopped going out on dates or to the dancing parties. I could hardly wait to get back to see her at Christmas. Besides being lovesick, my basketball career started to go south. The varsity from the year before had some players that Dudey felt he had to give a chance, and another real light-skinned Negro, Dick Ricketts, came to play. I think his team won the Pennsylvania High School Championship, defeating the great Wilt Chamberlain's team. The NCAA rules changed that year so that freshmen could play varsity. Dick was 6'8" and had an outside shot. Jim Tucker was 6'7" center. Dick was a high school parade All American. Dudey promised that he would start and that he would take his brother the next year, as well as Iver Izzo, a guard on his Pottsdown basketball team. Dudey honored these commitments. Moreover, to appease the bigots, he wouldn't start more than two Negroes. The underlying fact was that Pittsburgh was for the most part a blue collar, red neck town in which Duquesne alumni did not want more than two blacks staring in the first five. So I became a sub, even though in practice none of them outscored me or out-rebounded me. They were good shooters and played well together. We had a good team; we were invited to Madison Square Garden in NYC to the then much bigger NIT, which were 16 elite teams. We came in 4th and went to the NCAA championship, played in Chicago Stadium, beat Princeton, and lost to the University of Illinois in the Sweet Sixteen game.

Socially, one of the nice aspects of the year was that Ricketts invited me and Tucker down to Pottstown, Pennsylvania to meet his family. Now

Ricketts in a photograph looked exactly as if he were white, and he could have passed for white any day of the week. Because of my previous experiences with light-skinned people, I shied away from Ricketts, but I couldn't resist a weekend off campus. What a surprise I had when I met Dick's parents. Mr. Ricketts was light-skinned and an absolute saint. He was athletic director of a community center where Dick and his brother Dave could shoot baskets any hour of the day or night, and boy, could they shoot, including their father. Mrs. Ricketts turned out to be Irish and a total angel. We had a wonderful time. On the way back from Pittsburgh, I told Dick how comfortable and relaxed I felt in his mother's house.

He asked, "Didn't I expect to be at ease in his home?"

I replied, "Well, I imagined light-skinned Negroes spent most of their time at home talking down blacks. In short, I thought you all thought you were better than black Negroes."

Dick said, "You mean you thought you knew what we thought?"

Reflecting on what Dick had said pointed out what an outrageous assumption that was. Actually this was the second important lesson I had learned from Dick. The first was that when he came to Duquesne, he said that if he didn't start on the varsity team, he wouldn't stay, and if he left, it would be Duquesne's loss, because he was good and could play anywhere. Cocky? No. Just confident and full of a sense of his worth.

Unfortunately, that year Jim Tucker was suspended because someone had reported seeing two white girls together coming out of Tucker's room late at night. The Holy Fathers raised holy hell and suspended him for one semester. With Tucker out, I was allowed to play. I averaged 12.5 points a game and was the leading rebounder. We won the first Holiday Festival and Madison Square Garden at Christmas. We had a game at Chicago Stadium again against Ray Meyers' De Paul team for the right to play in the NIT. What a night that was. The stadium was standing room only: 17,000 to 20,000 people. Tucker had returned from his infamous suspension. I was still starting because Tucker, who was our leading scorer as a sophomore and who in one game had scored 42 points, was now playing tentatively and unsure of himself.

Tucker was a great leaper, but I could jump higher, and instead of jumping in one big jump, as he did, I had the ability to jump from one side of the basket to the other, usually getting a piece of the offensive rebound if I didn't top it in. Anyway, we started fast, and we were up by ten points or so at the end of the first quarter. By so doing, we locked out the effect of the huge, usually noisy home crowd. Early in the second quarter, I leaped to get a high rebound, and turning in the air I fed an outlet pass that resulted in a fast break score. While I was still in the air, and everyone's eyes, including the referee's, were glued on the flight of the ball and players speeding toward the basket, my opposing forward buried a fist deep in my gut. I pulled myself off the ground and followed him up the court, catching up. I said, "So now we are throwing punches?" He said, "Hey, tar baby, are you a cry baby too?" Vicious rebounding ensued as we ripped into each other. Suddenly I had two quick fouls and found myself sitting next to the coach, who was saying, "What the hell is going on out there?"

De Paul had become extremely physical, and since neither Tucker nor Ricketts were very physical, I found myself right back in the game. I tried to ignore the jibes and banged away at the boards, but after a particularly fierce exchange, I said, "Hey, if you want to fight, I'll see you outside." Sneering, he replied, "No niggers in no alleys, 'cause they all carry knives." I chased him, but I could not catch him, so I waited until he set a pick for an outside shot. I faked trying to get by him and instead raked him across the chops with a tremendous forearm, which left him sprawled on the floor and me with my third foul. When I returned to the bench, the coach would not speak to me.

It was half time, and the coach was screaming and throwing oranges around the locker room. I was still pissed and anxious to get back out there and crack that cat again. As if out of a fog, I heard, "And Johnson, can you tell me what the score is?" "We are down six," I stuttered. He looked at me and said, "Now what's going on with you and what's his name?"

"He's calling me nigger boy, tar baby, and a whole bunch of stuff."

"Silence, idiot, I am going to call you some names myself if you don't stop fouling and get us some rebounds. Like you don't know what's at stake here? National ratings and an invitation to the best post-season tournament, the NIT in Madison Square Garden. They can't beat you physically, so they are irritating you to get you out of the game. Wake up. This game is not over and you can still win it. Life is that way. People will do whatever they can to win, one way or another. If you let people make you mad to the point that you cannot function, you will be the loser, not them."

Second half was bitterly contested. I was mulling over the things the coach had said, and as usual I was sweating as if I had just stepped from a shower. We were in line up for a foul shot, when some of my sweat fell on the white player who had been calling me names. He said, "Don't drip that wet shit all over me, 'cause I might get stained black." Since it was so outrageous, I looked at him and laughed. He looked at me as if he thought I was crazy. I started chasing him around the court, not to hit him, but to rub the sweat on him, all over the court, whether he had the ball or not. I was all over him like a blanket. I kept telling him, "You're staining, man, staining, you're going to be black before the night's over." My laughter destroyed him. His concentration cracked 'cause he was no longer in control, and we came back to win the game for Duquesne. That year we came in third in the NIT. I was second highest rebounder scorer.

That episode of mine and so many other racial incidents that happened back in those days! Only one or two players could play if they were black. Now all the teams are almost seventy to eighty percent black, Sherman White told me a story one time about being out in Arizona with Claire Bee, and it was the first time that blacks had played out in Arizona, and they were in one of those field houses out there and LeRoy Smith was a real spirited ball player who had a fantastic jump shot. If he didn't jump over you, he drove over you. He was a powerfully built 6'2" black guard. He came on and drove over some white kid from Arizona and the place went up into a riot. Before the riot even started, the black kids had to stay in separate hotels and eat in the kitchen on campus. It was just a sign of the times. Sherman and his gang had to fight their way to the locker rooms, and then they had to barricade themselves there. Sherman went to Claire Bee and said, "Hey do something! Do something!" Claire Bee looked at him and said, "Hey Sherman, I'm a sick man."

That was also the year I switched from Army ROTC to Air Force ROTC, because when I went to sign up for my second year, the recruiting officer in the hall said that the Duquesne Army ROTC had been awarded a special honor. They would ship out with all of Western Pennsylvania's troops to the front line in Korea as soon as we graduated. Though I was only a sophomore and had two more years to go, I thought it prudent to switch to the Air Force ROTC, which I wasted no time in doing.

Summer brought me back to Englewood and Charlie Hunton's plastic factory. The dirt yard games were not as interesting, because Sherman was in jail, but my brother Alexander was All State in New Jersey and was going to the University of Connecticut on a basketball scholarship, and David to Youngstown on a football scholarship, and my brother Bob was twelve or thirteen, so we, the brothers Johnson, took on the world. We enjoyed playing and winning together.

Terry and I continued to see each other. That became difficult because she didn't want me to go home, and my mother was upset because I was away at school all winter and at Terry's house all summer. Terry's mother had jobs for me to do around the house. There were dishes, pots and pans to wash or dry. There was furniture to be moved, lawns to be mowed, and the garden to be weeded. Rooms to be pained inside and a porch to be painted outside. It was a hard-working family, and if I wanted to be around, I had better participate. Terry's mother was a beautiful black lady, whom I loved, but she worked herself to the bone to see that Terry got everything she wanted, especially clothes. Terry worked at Macy's in the crystal glass department as a saleslady, and she was proud, as she had every right to be, for in that summer of 1953 that was a position of high employment for a Negro. In those days they had a saying: That's a nigger's job, janitor, garbage man, maid and so on. She cherished her job and spent the vast majority of her salary on clothes, so she would look good on the job and at school.

Part of my duty in the courting of Terry was to pick her up after work, which meant I had to finish my work, take a bus and subway ride down to Macy's in New York, and bring her back to Englewood. Accomplishing this task with a certain amount of agility, it slowly came through to me that I was being domesticated and largely taken for granted. Even when Terry and I were going to a show in the city, she had to first come home and then go back into the city. Terry didn't like small town movies, but rather Broadway plays. That summer we saw Ondine with Audrey Hepburn, South Pacific with Mary Martin, and the King and I, not to mention concerts and off-Broadway shows.

On one occasion, we were coming back from a show and a late dinner at McGinnis' Restaurant. Entering the subway from the 42nd street side of the 8th avenue line, we came midway down the stairs to an open florist's shop. There leaning in the frame of the door was a black man with a store employee linen jacket on. Terry turned to me and said, in a loud voice, "Do you see how he is looking at me? He is looking me up and down. Why I do believe he is trying to look up my dress." I looked at the man and he leered at me with a sneer spreading over his face. I walked slowly down the stairs toward him, not knowing what to do or say. As I reached him, he faded into the interior of the florist's shop, where he backed up to a drawer and without taking his eyes off me, his right hand came up with a snub-nosed .38 caliber revolver, which he stuck right in my face.

"Get outta here or I'll blow your damn brains out," he said. "I'll blow your f—king brains out if you don't" I was a hero, but I wasn't going anywhere, because I was too scared to move. So I just stood there with a blank expression on my face, wondering if I would get to hear the explosion of the gun going off. Suddenly, he scooted past me onto the stairs, where he started jumping up and down, waving his gun in the air and shouting "Help, Help, I'm being robbed." I walked past him, whispering, hissingly, "asshole." I went down the stairs without as much as a glance at Terry as she came stumbling down behind me. I was just getting over my fright, while we were waiting for the uptown "A" train in stony silence, when suddenly this man burst onto the subway platform followed by two police officers. "There he is! There he is!" he screeched, pointing a finger at me.

"Listen, son," one of the police questioned me, "Did you try to rob this man?" I did not open my mouth but gritted my teeth looked straight into their eyes and shook my head NO. "Show me your wallet," he demanded. After going through my papers, he said, "OK, if you didn't try to rob him, what did happen?" I simply glared at my accuser, but I did not open my mouth. "OK, the officer said, "If you are not going to talk, I am going to take you in." As he started to grab my arm, Terry piped up, "He was protecting me." "Ah," the officer said, looking at Terry. "What was he protecting you from?"

Terry stammered, "We were coming down the stairs and this man came out and stared me up and down in a nasty way and tried to look up my dress."

"Well," the officer said, thinking for a while, "He didn't say anything, did he? He didn't touch you, did he? We can't arrest him for looking, but we're going to have a long talk with him, and as for you, son, other people looking at your woman ain't worth dying over. Why don't you go back to New Jersey real peaceful like."

It was an awkward quiet that enveloped us on our return trip home. When we arrived at Terry's I made sure she got in OK. Then I walked home instead of waiting for the bus, shaken but happy to be alive as I replayed that gun scene over and over in my mind. Everything went downhill from then. The summer ended, and I was trying to stop eating out and going to New York in order to save money to buy clothes to return to school. That prompted me to say one night, "Why don't we go to the local movies?" As we boarded the bus to go from Teaneck to downtown Englewood, I reminded her that we did not have enough money for the return bus fare if we bought popcorn. Once on board, though, we lapsed into one of our frequent arguments. They were usually over quickly, and then I lapsed back into service of her majesty.

Gretchen and Grace

After we lost the NIT the next year, we came back to Pittsburgh. The people at Duquesne were good to us. Five thousand people met us at the airport, even though we had lost to the Holy Cross team of 1954 led by Tommy Heinz. We shot just 16% instead of our normal 40%. I really felt bad about starting because Tommy Heinz physically put Ricketts and Tucker away. While they were good shooters, they were not aggressive on the back board. Without the basketball, Duquesne could not win. At the NIT, I broke my engagement with Terry. That was in March. I told her I was going out with Gretchen. Terry laughed at me and said that white girl would never take me seriously, that it would never work out, and that I would come crawling back to her.

That junior year was my best year. I was All-Catholic, All-American honorable mention, All-Tristate, All-Pennsylvania Player of the Week several times. Senior year I did not get a chance to star. Still I was honorable mention in All-Catholic and All-American, the best sixth man in the United States, and All-Eastern, All-Pennsylvania and All-Tristate.

I had seen Gretchen at the airport on a return from an earlier game. Her big almond-shaped eyes, her chocolate brown eyes, velvety and set off in a sea of buttermilk. She was a picture of joy and happiness. She made no special effort to come forward and greet me. She stayed in the crowd and we exchanged glances only. That moment at the airport was the beginning of our relationship, with crowds of people around and just our glances, which were the only sign of real feeling for each other, so far as anyone outside ourselves could discern. Going back to my daily university activities, trying to glean an education was routine until Gretchen started calling and suggesting that I learn bridge in the student lounge. It was with this pretext of learning bridge that I began to meet her in the student lounge after classes, and she taught me to play bridge, and how to waltz and tango. She sent me records of classical music to listen to. She suggested reading the good authors, and she taught me how to drive. She got her father's car and came up to the bluff, where I would hop into the car and she would drive out to the woods. We talked, and what we found out was that I, being black, and contrary to popular belief, was not a person with two heads, or incapable of learning, or a sex maniac. I learned that white people could be tender and that white girls could be lovable. Having been denied any real white relationships or friendships up to this point and having it built into our society that the black is the second class citizen, it was flattering and ego-inflating and beautiful for that white girl to follow me around, arrange our secret meetings, and to spend moments of her time with me. In the space from Christmas to Easter we saw many things together. We went to concerts, but never together. I would meet her, sit beside her, and never speak to her during concerts. I would meet her in the movies and only in the shadow of the movie darkness would we kiss one another.

We went to friends' houses where there were a number of people, though not a great number, who realized that we really liked and perhaps loved one another. Those people allowed us to come into their homes. We never betrayed or deceived them in any way. We never had any real sex between us. Gretchen then told me that she wanted to tell everybody how she felt about me at the university and that we should go out in public and stop sneaking around. Well, if that's what she wanted, I would do it. So we started to date and to go out publicly together. From being the most popular athlete on campus, I became a pariah who was dating a white girl. It started the most notorious splitting and polarization of the campus that I ever knew about. She was called names. I was talked about, never to my face, but talked about by the student body. The vast majority were against our relationship. The only person who would talk to me was Mrs. Farley, my advisor, who told me this was not the thing to do, that we were only going to hurt one another, that we were destroying the school, and that the school was in two hostile camps.

I was called in by Mrs. Kiley, who was a friend who had steered me through the education department. She was about 40 years old, and when I walked in, she was crying. She said, "Oh Fletcher, how could you destroy everything that you worked so hard for? All the people loved you, and now they hate you! It doesn't make sense to throw your life away like that. You have a beautiful girlfriend named Terry. Why don't you go back to her and leave this other girl alone. There must be something not right with Gretchen." I asked her if she knew Gretchen, and she could not say she did, because Gretchen was in the school of arts and sciences. So I asked her to meet with

Gretchen and see how she felt about her. Well, Mrs. Kiley met with her and said she liked Gretchen and that she could understand how we liked each other, because we were both easy-going. But the world was not ready for us. And again she cried. I said we did not know what we were going to do, but that we would think about it.

The school authorities, who were the Holy Ghost Fathers, found out about our clandestine meetings and imagined all sorts of sex orgies that never took place. The school wrote to Gretchen's parents and said she was dating a black Negro student called Fletcher Johnson and that this only pointed out her immaturity, and that it was the school's opinion that she was too immature to be part of any part of Duquesne's student life, and she was therefore suspended. Gretchen was immediately called home by her mother and father, who insisted on keeping her there. We communicated only through an aunt, who was a nun, whom Gretchen was allowed to call.

One blustering, cold day in March, Gretchen's mother and Gretchen came to the bluff and telephoned me in the dormitory. It was a Saturday. I came down and spoke to the two of them in the car. Gretchen's mother wanted to meet me, see what I was like, and talk to us about our predicament. After having met me, she said she could see why Gretchen liked me, and she asked us if we didn't think we could, each of us, find people of our own races to associate with and marry. Couldn't we see all the hardships that we were causing the people in our circles? Our response was that we hadn't really thought about it. We had just developed a very close friendship with a lot of meaningful conversations, and we just loved being near one another and would like to get married. Her mother started to cry and said, "Well, you are absolutely killing my husband. He has a heart problem, and he had a heart attack as soon as he heard about you and Gretchen. It is the most terrible thing to see someone you love about to die."

I said, "But we don't want to hurt people; we are not that type. It is just that we fell in love, and we would like to be correct and end the love in the way we were taught. That is to marry one another and have children." Gretchen's mother said, "that takes strength from my husband, and I cannot give consent for such a wedding." I said that in the Bible it says that people who get married should cleave unto themselves and cleave from their families so that they are their own separate families. I thought Gretchen and I could do this. Well, her mother really started to cry, and Gretchen said, "Oh Fletcher, you do not have to make her cry." I thought that if she could not see the truth in what I had been saying about the problem, then Gretchen would probably weaken in the face of the onslaught of society against our wedding. Her mother continued to cry for a while, and then she eventually got herself together, and she said, "If you could only give us three or five more years, then we would not contest the wedding, and we would consent to whatever it is you would like to do. But we would like you not see each other for three years, and then, if at the end of three years you really love each other and want to see each other, then my husband and I will consent to your wedding. I said that was impossible, and I would not wait for three years to see Gretchen. Then her mother started to cry again, and Gretchen started to cry. I said, "Gretchen, what do you want? Whatever you want, that is what I am willing to do."

Gretchen said, "I don't want my mother to cry, and I am tired of all the hurt and trouble that I am creating." I said that I could consent to a one-year separation, and at the end of that time we either got married or we forgot about the whole thing." Then I watched as Gretchen and her mother dried their tears. We agreed that would be an acceptable solution. Gretchen's mother got out of the car and went into the student union building. Gretchen and I drove around for about an hour and a half and talked about how sad it was that the world could not see how we felt about one another, and how hard it is to swim against the stream and all the forces that make up our racist society. We decided that I would go back to New Jersey and teach school or go into the service, whichever came up first, and she would go back to Patton, Pennsylvania with her parents, and we would not see each other for one year. We kissed and fondled each other. We had never had a sexual relationship; we were saving it for our wedding night. We talked about how that would be the one thing that would really prove that we loved each other, if we could really wait until we were married before we did anything sexual. We went back to the bluff, picked up her mother, and there we parted.

The Gretchen affair kept me on the bench and probably cost us the NIT that year. That was not the only repercussion in the tri-state area of Ohio, West Virginia and Pennsylvania. Duquesne's Holy Ghost Fathers decided they would not have any more black players on their teams. They did this by cutting back on scholarships, and if my memory serves me correctly, it was some ten years before they had another black basketball player. That is to say, they stopped recruiting black players, though there were some on the GI Bill or who came to Duquesne for their educations without scholarships. It was a good ten to fifteen years before they had another good basketball team after Dick Ricketts left the bluff. With the departure of Gretchen the school seemed to quiet down, and the people who had been angry at me became friendly again. The members of the basketball team became friendly, too, to the point that I thought that everyone was being guilty for the manner in which they had treated me and Gretchen.

It was a four-month relationship that was really Platonic. There was heavy petting, but nothing more than that. A great deal of the time we spent talking about Catholicism. She made a real Catholic believer out of me. After she left, I was in a deep depression, which I remedied by just plain hard work. I made the Dean's list that semester. The rest of the school year went by in a benign manner with nothing really going on other than people trying to mend fences with me. Now that I was on my way back to Englewood, I had to tell Terry that I no longer loved her and there was no reason for us to get married in June as we had previously planned. I thought about the way her mother had placed her on a pedestal. She was a vain person who expected gifts as if they were things that should be automatically given to her. So when I walked in and talked to her mother it was ironic that her mothing started talking about the wedding that was going to be in June when I graduated, because we had been engaged for two and one half years. She had already decided that we were going to live across the street in a development of some houses that I would have to make a down payment on, and that I could live in with them and pay so much rent a month until we had money for the down payment. Even though after I had told Terry the engagement was off, and we had not exchanged one letter in months, it was taken for granted that everything was all right.

I waited until her mother had gone upstairs, and then I said to Terry, "I am sorry, but I have to tell you I am going to call off the wedding because I have been dating another girl. I am not sure about how I definitely feel at this point, and I am going to wait one year before I make any kind of decisions. Therefore, you are free to do and go out with whomever you please." She looked at me and just could not believe it, that I could have found someone else to go out with. I had been out at Duquesne for almost four years and I had been 99% to 100% loyal to Terry. There were times when I went out and did the things that I had to do, but I was loyal in my love for Terry. It was only with this last incident that everything was put into focus, and that I found Terry to be vain, egotistical, and that she had taken me for granted. I left, and the next day her mother called and spoke to me. She said, "Don't you think you and Terry should get together, and don't you want to see her again before you leave?" So I went over again, and I spoke to Terry's stepfather and to her mother, and they all felt that I had put this girl off for two and one half years, and I had bought a ring for her and I should go ahead and get married in June because everyone was expecting it.

Terry and I stayed after her mother and stepfather had gone upstairs, and she asked, "Who is this other girl?" I told her that her name was Gretchen. She said, "Gretchen. Is that a white girl?" I said, "Yes, she is white." Then she said, "You will be an absolute fool! No white girl is going to marry you, and she is not coming back to you, not ever! You want to break up our relationship and cause me all this pain and trouble for something that is never going to be any good. Black men have always loved white women, and the women go out, and they do not marry you, and if you do get married, you will never have a good time. It will always be a bad thing." She said to me, "You are being a complete ass, and no white woman is going to marry you, so why don't you forget the whole thing, and let's get married in June."

I said to her, "Terry, I do not care if I marry the girl or not, but one thing certain is that I am not going to marry you, and I am not going to be dictated to by society. I closed my eyes to a whole race of people before, and now I am not dealing with races anymore but with individuals, and I do not care how people feel or how they think about me. I have to be true to myself." Then I left, and Terry was still laughing and saying I was just a fool. I went back to Duquesne at the end of Easter Vacation, and dug into my books with a vengeance. Some of the professors had said that they were going to put me out of school for going out with Gretchen, but I managed to get all A's that last semester.

When graduation finally came at the Syrian Mosque, there were thousands of people there, and though I had told Terry not to come down for graduation, she nonetheless saw fit to come. She came, bringing her aunt and uncle, her mother and stepfather, and her brother. My mother and father came with all my brothers and sisters, and I was happy to see them. My brother Alexander was just back from Korea. I told Terry again that it was over and thanked her for coming down. As soon as graduation was over, and I was walking out of the Syrian Mosque, Gretchen appeared out of nowhere, grabbed me, and kissed me full on the lips. As soon as she did that, I heard the most God-awful wailing that you can imaging, as if on signal and synchronized, my mother started crying, Terry's mother started crying, Terry started crying, my sister Ruth started crying, my sister Alice started crying, and Terry's aunt started crying. They were all crying and wailing like a Baptist reunion. Gretchen and I looked at them, and then Gretchen started crying. She ran out, and I ran after her. When I caught up with her, we took a ride in her car and stayed away for an hour or so. After we returned, the graduation had ended, and my family was waiting for me to come back, as was Terry and her family. They all cried as I got out of the car and Gretchen drove off. Gretchen and I had decided that our relationship was making so many people unhappy that maybe we shouldn't write each other 'til the end of the year.

My mother was saying, "Junior, how could you?"

I got into the car and rode back to the university and put all my things into Daddy's car, and we all got into a caravan. When we stopped for gas on the Pennsylvania Turnpike, Terry came and got in my car and started crying and asking me, "How could you do that? How could you treat me so bad?" I reminded her that she had told me she didn't care what I did, and that she knew I would come crawling back to her because this white girl would not have me, but she didn't want to hear that. She continued to cry and scream until when we were at Harrisburg, about 200 miles from Pittsburgh, I jumped out of the car and told my father he could take me to the railroad station or leave me on the highway, but I definitely was not going back to Englewood. So my father drove me to the train station, and I took a train to Pittsburgh without any baggage. When I got back to Pittsburgh, I stayed a night at the "Y" and the next day I got a room near the campus and a job at the Fort Pitt Brewery, which immediately assigned me to public relations work canvassing all the black bars in a four-state area. I did not drink any alcohol. I did not smoke, either, and I thought this a crazy type of job. The people in the bars knew that I was a national figure, so I told them I was in training and was going to play professional basketball. If I had a drink at every place I stopped, I'd be drunk before the day was over and couldn't work. They accepted that, and over the summer I got the brewery 81 or 82 new customers. Soon I was promoted to going to all bars, white, Puerto Rican, and everything else. My white friend Mr. Howell, who had promised to help me, wrote me a check to buy a car, which I repaid.

I had a lot of strange experiences. Down in Youngstown, Ohio, I told one of the black bosses I met about my predicament with Terry and Gretchen. He said to me, "Look, Fletcher, you know this is 1954, and there is no way you can go out with a white girl, let alone marry one." At that time the Supreme Court was just getting ready to make the decision on school desegregation. There was a lot of racial tension all over the country. He said to me, "If you marry this white girl, as black as you are, what will happen is that every time an arrow is shot into the air, no matter if you hide under a rock or swim in the ocean, that arrow will come down and hit you in the ass, as if radar controlled. There is no way you can expect to have a happy life in that sort of situation." Those words were more profound than they seemed on the surface.

I was a hermit for about three months, then I started to go back to the bluff to the student union to see all the students that had come back after summer vacation. I was still accepted because I had just graduated the year before. I started to go to parties and whatnot. There was this one girl who seemed to be every place that I was. Her mother owned a disc jockey program. One night she asked me if I would come to a party. I went to the party, and we had a good time in her home. As the party was ending she took everyone to the local Elks, where there was a band and people were dancing. This other girl walked up to me and said, "So how is Green doing?" I said, "He must be back. He was my roommate last year, but I'm not on campus now. I have to work." I was kind of gruff. Then I thought, why am I being mean to this girl? So after a while I asked her if she wanted to dance, and she was a fantastic dancer and was beautiful. Looking closely at her, I recognized that I had met her the year before with my roommate outside Duquesne Gardens after a game. Her movements were lithe. She reminded me of some beautiful black panther moving along a jungle trail. Her name was Grace, and she was really graceful. I asked her if she wanted a ride home. She did, and her home was in a very nice area in which I thought no blacks lived. Then she said, "This is my house."

We parked in the driveway. It had been months since I had been with anybody, and it had been an even longer time since I had been really relaxed with someone. There were no tensions from stares or glares from society because of a black-white union. There was no sense of doing something sneaky or contrived or unacceptable to the general public. I was really relieved and happy to be with Grace. We kissed and I jumped all over her and tried to make love to her in the car. I wrestled with her, and she escaped by jumping out of the car and running into the house. I sat there for a while, just a little bit flustered, and at first a bit pissed off. I felt that I had been enticed, and then I blamed myself for staying away from sex for so long. I became ashamed for having thrown myself on Grace. So I drove off, feeling the complete heel. The next morning, I left Pittsburgh and went out to Youngstown, where I stayed for three weeks selling beer and doing public relations work in the different distribution houses for the Fort Pitt Brewery. Returning to the brewery one morning, I was at my desk arranging a presentation of what I had accomplished and the statistics of what had been sold, and who were the repeat customers, and I received a phone call.

The voice on the end of the phone said, "I would like to buy two cases of beer, because we are going to throw a lawn party." I said, "I'm sorry, but I sell beer by the train car and truck loads. Call your wholesale dealer, and he will be able to get you your Fort Pitt Beer. Thank you for calling." I was about to hang up when the voice said, "Don't you know who I am?" I said, "No, I'm sorry, I do not." She said, "I am Grace, the girl you were with the other night at the dance and took home." "Yeah," I said, "I'm sorry. I had been meaning to call you, but I couldn't find your number." I apologized for practically assaulting her in the car. I said that I was not really that bad a guy, and I really did not mean her any harm. I was just uptight a little bit. I asked her if we could go out to dinner, and I could show her that I could be a gentleman. She said OK, and I took her out to dinner. It was the calm that follows the storm. When we walked places, no one turned to stare or glare or make cutting and brutal remarks. There was no abrasive body English from the people we encountered. It was nice to be free and open and to have a worthwhile and meaningful relationship without society and all the authorities being against what you were trying to do. By that I mean the church, the police, the school, and people who directed those institutions.

I dated her more, and she was strange. She would sing to me in the car, and she cooked chicken. She went with me to play basketball, and to the theater. She was a great professional dancer. As a ballerina, she danced on the local educational Pittsburgh TV station. She was the first black to dance at the Nixon Theater in downtown Pittsburgh. She won many awards for dancing, and she was going to take off with a Black troupe to dance through Europe. She was definitely more intellectual and brighter than I. Grace had come from a very poor family, and she had been born on the north side of Pittsburgh. Her mother had died when Grace was five years old, and her father had left her and her two brothers with his sister. He ran off with a white woman to live in the Bronx, and he later had another six or so children. He never sent money regularly to support his children in Pittsburgh, so when Grace was about twelve, she answered an ad to babysit the children of a family named Sherman. They liked her and took her into their home as a live-in babysitter from the time she was 12 until she was 17. The dressed her in nice clothes, sent her to school, and to tennis and ballet lessons. She also went to summer camp. She became a member of the family. The Shermans, who were Jewish, brought her up as a rich Jewish girl.

Pro-Basketball and the Air Force

That September I went off to try out for basketball teams, and at that point I quit my job with the beer company. I was drafted by the Syracuse Nationals, even though I was a sixth man. I was the only sixth man in the country who was drafted by one of the then eight professional teams. I had finished my senior year as the fourth highest scorer on the Duquesne team and the third highest rebounder. Still, there were only slots for 70 to 80 pro players in the whole United States. I went up to Syracuse, though I still had an obligation to the ROTC. I was in the Air Force ROTC and became a second lieutenant upon graduation. At that time, the Air Force was overloaded with second lieutenants, and the Korean War was winding down, so they were not commissioning all the new graduates. They kept me on call for induction. At Syracuse I did well. I rebounded as well as anybody in camp and much better all-around than most, though there were at least five or six guys who were taller. I earned the name of the beast with ten fingers. That team went on to win the NBA Championship. We had Red Rocca, Earl Boyd, Wally Ostrinoff, Paul Seymour, and George King. Al Servey was the coach-player, and we really liked one another. George liked the kind of "Wild Man from Borneo" basketball that I played, and the fact that I could get my fingers on almost anything that went out, be it offensive or defensive. I had a real shot at making the team.

I remember one real class basketball player. His name was Dolph Schayes, and he was holding out for a $20,000 contract. Base pay at that time was $7500 per man, though at the time I am writing this, the average income of an NBA player is $100,000. When Dolph, who was All-Pro and All-American, came back to the team, I was cut and went down to the Baltimore team. Claire Bee was coach of the Baltimore Bullets at that time, and Ray Felix and Uplinger were the outstanding players. I played one game for them in Hershey, Pennsylvania, against a Philadelphia club that had Joe Faulks, Max Oslofsky, Neil Johnson, and Paul Aron. I scored nine points, but the money for that team was running out, so they kept only seven or eight players at a time on pay. After that I went back to work at the brewery. Weekends I played in the Eastern League for the Westborough Barons in Pennsylvania. Grace drove out with me on those weekends. We shared chicken in the car as we drove the 800-mile round trip through blizzards. I was making good money, I was still playing basketball, and I was carefree until one Saturday night when my little Ford, with slick old tires, slid on a back road in the mountains. I slid into the woods and into a little brook. A couple of farmers came and pulled me out with a horse and a chain. I asked Sheldon Brown, an optometrist in the Westborough area, to come down and take me to the game. I had been driving a thousand miles a week doing promotional work and a thousand miles every weekend. I got into that game one quarter late, scored twenty points, and we won. Eddy White, the coach, was unsatisfied. He said I should have arrived earlier, and that if I couldn't do better, he would have to find someone else. I thought God had spared me in the accident and that I was lucky to be there. So I told him, "Please get somebody else." He did.

The next week, I showed up at the Willkes Barre Armory, but this time in a Scranton Minor uniform. We went in and beat those Wilkes Barre players, Floyd Lane, Ed Bronan and me. With about three minutes to go, we were ahead by eight points. Ed White sent in the Dankus brothers, who were football players about 6'6" tall. They weren't good shooters, but they were what you'd call hatchet men. I had been shooting deep shots from the corner, and they were falling in. I saw these two guys come in, and I knew what they were for. We lined up on the side of the foul line, and I knew that one of them was going to chop my legs out, and the other was going to hit me from above and nail me to the ground. So as the foul shot went up, I knocked the one guy down with my right elbow and spun around behind the one closer to the basket and pushed him behind me. I got the rebound and passed it off. I started down the court and heard the crowd yelling, but I didn't know what they were yelling about. When I turned around there was this fist flying at me. It was one of the Durkan brothers, and he threw a right hand over punch, and his momentum was coming toward me, so I just ducked down, and he rode up on my shoulders. I did a full press with him and crashed him to the floor on his head and right shoulder, and when I got him up in the air, from that crowd of eight or nine thousand, there was the most devastating hush you ever heard. They all seemed to gasp in unison as he and his head sped to the ground. The other brother came out, and I flattened him. I started knocking people to the ground right and left, the stands emptied, and the Minors were chasing me around the floor. They pulled my uniform off. The police were trying to get me, and we finally fought our way to the locker room. They wouldn't let me come back out and play, but the team finally went out after half an hour, and everything was cleared up. Of course the Westborough team went on to win and we lost the league championship. The basketball season ended.

I went back to work. After I had gone out to Youngstown for about two weeks of promotion, I got a telephone call in my room from Grace. She said, "Come and get me. I'm at the Shermans." I said, "What's up?" She said, "Well come and get me and I will tell you all about it." So I drove out to the Sherman's house and Grace was standing in front of the driveway with all her suitcases and bags, and some clothes thrown over her arms. She told me she had gotten into an argument with Mrs. Sherman, and Mrs. Sherman had said that either Grace had to stop seeing me or she would have to leave. I asked her what that was all about, and Grace said it was about me bringing her back late. I promised to bring her back on time, but she decided that if she had to choose between me and living at the Shermans' house, she was choosing me. "I'm going over to the north side. I'm going to live with my aunt from now on." We packed everything in my car and drove across Pittsburgh to the north side. As we drove, I became increasingly somber and alarmed as the housing got worse the further we went. When we came to the last house on her street, and the worst house on the street, that was her aunt's house. It was poorly lit. I went into the house to find the aunt with a large bottle of wine in the kitchen, with three fellows, none of them her husband, playing cards. She was surprised to see Grace and gave her a room upstairs. The floor was patched linoleum, and an electric heater was burning. Here Grace had just come from living for five or six years in a large Colonial with a lot of grounds, a maid and a cook, and her own bedroom. All the affluent things one finds in a wealthy Jewish home and all the education that she had acquired. And now she was suddenly dealt into this situation that was a tremendous comedown. I felt terribly responsible and obligated to do something about it.

I started to look for a place for her to stay. My landlord, Mr. Parker, said he simply couldn't have a girl living in an all-male apartment building, and that I would have to find someplace else. So I looked around the hill district until I found a nice church going family who gave us two rooms in their house. One room up front was for Grace, and I had a room in the back. The Ramseys, who owned the house, allowed Grace to visit my room, but when it was late at night they kept using the bathroom outside just to let us know that if she was in my room, she should go back to her room. I always sent her back, even though we slept together.

Finally, I got my orders to report to Roslyn Air Force Base. I asked Grace to marry me, because I thought that I wouldn't find anyone whom I thought I could get along with as well as I got along with her. I thought that as a black person in this society, there was no need to continue waiting for Gretchen. I felt indebted to Gretchen, but I loved Grace. Before I made up my mind, I took Grace out to Youngstown with me to have our astronomical signs read by this old lady. The lady told me that our marriage could never work, that we should not get married, and that our signs were incompatible. Grace and I laughed at that and become more determined than ever to be married. We did the day before I went into the service.

We fought the night before and almost didn't get married because I had to do everything. We had to arrange for transportation for her brides-maid. I arranged the wedding, paid for the reception, and got my best friend Howell to take her father's place and give her away. My brother was coming in from Korea. I had made all these arrangements and thought, "one more thing to do! Don't you think this girl, the bridesmaid, can arrange for her own ride without one of us picking her up?" Her family wouldn't come to the wedding. Her father couldn't be reached; he was supposedly a lawyer in New York City, though I thought he worked for the post office. Later we found out one winter when we went up to NYC on one of the weekends that I was playing basketball there, that he had been lying and was in fact doing odds and ends kind of work and that his wife, Shirley, was working for the telephone company. No one in her family did anything towards helping her to get married or even seemed vaguely interested as to whether she got married. It was a very poor relationship that family had, which made me feel even more obligated to go ahead with the marriage and get her out of Pittsburgh. I thought that if I returned to Gretchen after a year, all kinds of bad things would happen to Grace.

After the wedding, there was a party thrown by Mr. Joe Aiken at the Brewery, and we then went out to the Green Meadow Motel on Route 22 and stayed there the night of our honeymoon. Grace got angry because Sherman had joined a club and had planned a dancing party for us that night, and I thought we could stop in and say hi. She got upset about that and probably had every right to. Then the next day we got lost going into Long Island. We had a huge argument in the car about my ability to read road maps. From day one, we had a stormy relationship with tremendous highs and fantastic lows. I was not sure she was ready for marriage, but then she would sing a song and we would dance, and that would erase all the morbid and depress-ing thoughts about her and her personality. Well, we finally found the base.

The day I went into the service was May 15, 1955, and that summer we started right away to practice basketball, because General McCauley was interested in having a team that would beat the Andrews Air Force Base team. The general arranged for us to have a two-bedroom place in the visiting officer's quarters, with our own bathroom and an orderly to take care of us at $5.00 a month until I could afford an apartment. The general also arranged a job for Grace, a civilian job, because she was a great typist, though she had dropped out of Duquesne after we started seeing one another. She had not told me that. General McCauley had me eat at his table every day for the first year. He planned to build a team around me and one other player. Finally we got officer's living quarters over at Mitchell Air Force Base. I was appointed Provost Marshall, so I granted myself passes to take off on the weekends and go play basketball in the mountains. Grace went along too, and we had a good time driving around and playing basketball. It was a carefree sort of life, without any real serious moments other than that we would win this game, or that championship, or that we might have to carry out some orders from superior officers. Everything was going along smoothly, and if I did not love Grace, I was coming to it.

The time had come for me to tell Gretchen that I was not waiting the year, and despite all the things we had gone through, I had gotten married, and I thought that was the best calculated risk for happiness. I had told Gracie about Terry and Gretchen, and my whole life. I got to the point where every day I would think about it a bit and wonder what Grace was doing and that I had to let her know that I was married. So I decided that I would write her a letter. I wrote her a many-paged letter describing the things that she and I had done together, and how happy we had been, and how much I really loved her, and about how I thought we two together was not a calculated risk for happiness. It was not the time for black-white marriages, and our children would suffer, and that didn't make sense. I told her I had found this girl that I loved and could be happy with, and I wished her the most happiness in the world. I told her that I would always love her in my own way and that she would always have some corner in my heart. I signed it and asked her to forgive me for any sadness I might have caused her, and that was it. I was going to send the letter, but I never, never got to send it. I could not bring myself to do it. I tried to figure out who I had the most alliance or allegiance to, and I came away thinking that I owed a great allegiance to Grace because I married her, and that if I sent this letter to Gretchen, she might use it to get back at me by showing it to Grace, and then Grace would be upset. The next day I thought about how Gretchen had put up with a lot. She got put out of school, humiliated and ostracized, both at the university and at home, and I owed her something better than a letter. I did not destroy the letter. So I was hung up with this indecision. As time went on, I did not do anything.

Finally, maybe a month or so later, Grace and I had enough money to move into an apartment. As we were moving, Grace came across this letter. She went absolutely bananas. She knew that I had dated this white girl because I had told her about it, but that did not sit too well with her. First, she had the experience of her father running off with a white lady and deserting her brothers and sisters, and now this letter to Gretchen. The only thing that she could see in the letter was that I was black and that was why I couldn't have this white girl. That's what she said. We argued and she left. After two or three hours I went out and found her crying. I said to her, "Grace, don't you understand that I could write you a letter and leave? What I did was tell this girl that she has a corner in my heart, but I left her for you." There were minutes of silence, and she said finally that she understood, and I got her back home. Within a month she was pregnant with our first child. She worked until her seventh month, and then we had a little girl. When she had the baby, I was not home. She had the baby on Saturday, and on Friday I had gone to Youngstown and Westminster College with my brother, whom I was helping to get a football, basketball and track scholarship. To make money, he came and lived with Grace and me, and he worked in a nearby steel yard of a pipe-fitting company.

Our Renee was a completely lovable and beautiful little girl. We carried on with our domestic life. Then one day when I was playing in the mountains with the Hazelton Hawks, I was talking with a guy named Eddy, and he said he had just gotten a full scholarship to dental school in Tennessee, and that his brother was studying at the University of Bologna in Italy. His brother had heard there was a team coming over to the United States to find a basketball player. The Italian Olympic Committee wanted six good American players to help improve their teams for the 1960 Olympic games, which were going to be held in Rome. Eddy wondered if I would be interested in his place, since he was going to stay in the US and go to dental school. He said he would introduce me to this Italian guy, and I thought that maybe I would get another shot at medicine.

After that famous letter, Grace and I had nights when she did not feel like sleeping with me. Any little thing would set her off. She treated me like someone who had deceived her and let her down, not someone to be trusted. Our relationship deteriorated insidiously and continuously from the moment she found that letter. It was an unchanging downhill course that was only momentarily interrupted by her becoming pregnant with our second child. He was a little boy who was later nicknamed Chino, and I loved him dearly. He was born eleven months after the first child. The first time I missed the birth because I had taken Alexander to Duquesne and Westminster looking for scholarships, and now this time I had taken my brother David to Youngstown to look for a football scholarship. For both moments of birth, I was not there. Grace felt that my family ties were too strong. She had a fixed hostility to me. She would have these moments when she was really a wonderful person to be around, but they became more and more rare as our years added up.

While I was in the Air Force, we had a lot of fun playing basketball, which was the thing I did most in my first year in the service. We had Joey McCoy, who was a 26th Division Air Force Commander. He had been shipped in from Andrews Air Force Base, which was known as a famous place for basketball players. That year Andrews had Cliff Hagen and other professional college athletes. They were loaded, and they were going for the northeastern title. They came up to Mitchell Air Force Base where we played, because our base was too small to have a gym. We had knocked off all the other teams, so we played for the championship with Andrews. Their team flew in on a big strategic air command plane. There was a round-robin trophy, and if you won it three years in a row, you got to keep it. It was supposed to be displayed in our gym, but our team never unpacked it, because it was felt that we would be defeated by Andrews. It was a two out of three series. On the first night, we beat them by six points or so. Cliff Hagen had 19 points and I had 28 points, and they were really surprised. The next night out, they got ahead of us 12 points, and there were about 15 minutes to go. We had only eight guys. We never had a full court practice, because our base was so small. Six of our guys were kids from high school that the two of us who had played in college coached into fairly good ball players.

We were tired, and it looked like we could not catch up, so I said, "If you cannot catch them, just don't give them baskets and don't chase them. Just score your baskets and let them run." And boy, did they ever run. They ran and they ran and they dunked and they yelled and they raised hell while they were beating us. They heckled and they jeered and they did all kinds of weird things. They beat us by maybe 30 points.

The final game was scheduled for the next night. Their commander came over and asked if we would play in the afternoon, so their team could get out to Bunker Hill, Indiana, where the world-wide Air Force tournament was being held that year. That way they would get a good night's sleep and be ready for the next series of games with the teams coming in from all over the world. We said, sure, we would play them in the afternoon. The next afternoon they came down, and they were rested, but not fantastically so. We were rested because we had not really run the night before. The game started and we jumped off to a ten-point lead, and we hung on like bulldogs. Finally, with two minutes to go, we were still sitting with a ten-point lead. Cliff Hagen went bananas, and one of our little men drove to the basket, and Cliff chopped him down brutally. Mike, our little guy, jumped off the ground, and Cliff started in with his right hand. Mike was about 5'8," and he must have weighed about 140 pounds. Cliff Hagen was 6'5" and he weighed about 220. I jumped in and grabbed Cliff. We wrestled, and I got him down on the ground, jumped off, and hit him with a couple of punches. He started trying to kick me, so I grabbed one of his feet and started dragging him around the gym. That precipitated a riot. Andrews Air Force Base had flown in a lot of supporters, mostly big officers. They all emptied onto the floor, and Mike came out, and there were many more of them than our eight players. Then our stands emptied and got into the riot. The Air Police came and clubbed a couple of people and got everyone back into their seats. We played out the last two minutes and beat them. We got to uncrate that trophy. We went to the worldwide tournament, but we were tired, I had a twisted ankle, and Don, the other college player had pulled a thigh muscle. Still, I made the All Air Force team as their #1 center. Back at Roslyn we came in second in the Eastern League, which was a professional league.

The next year in the Air Force was not as interesting, but we won the North Eastern tournament again. We didn't go to the worldwide tournament. Grace and I still had great ups and downs. We were Catholic, but I started to feel that Grace and I didn't have enough of a solid base to have any more children. We had to try to learn to get along with one another.

During those two years in the Air Force, I was instrumental in helping my brothers get scholarships at Connecticut University and the University of Youngstown. After basketball season and just prior to being discharged from the Air Force, a friend, Eddy Weiner, told me about an opportunity to go to Europe and play for an Italian basketball team. I had a contract to go back to Syracuse because the Baltimore team I had been with folded and the last NBA team I had been drafted by was Syracuse. Although they had the rights to me, they sold me down to the St. Louis Hawks, where I got to play with Cliff Hagen, with whom I had that tremendous fist fight. St. Louis, Missouri at that time was not a great place to be.

Martin Luther King's bus ride feat had just ended, and I had been one of the people invited to Englewood High School as one of the educated young blacks in Englewood to go and hear Martin Luther King, because he was being hailed as the new Mahatma Gandhi of the Black People of the United States. I went and listened to him, and he told how the bus boycott had worked, how it had been provoked by some black lady who had been asked to give up her seat to a white person in the deep South. I remember sitting in the balcony and listening to Martin Luther King talk about how he wanted peace in the United States and that by this kind of collective bargaining and boycotting we could achieve the equality needed to make the 1954 ruling on schools work. Afterwards, Dr. Leroy McCloud, the principal of Lincoln High School, who was the first black teacher at that school, which was 98% black, introduced me to Martin Luther King, and I told him that I was one of those rabble rousers that he had spoken about in his speech. At that time I was still pretty hot about not having a chance to play on the basketball court when the coach put me on the bench and all the other bad things that had happened with Gretchen. I believed in the law of Hamurabbi, which was "an eye for an eye" and that one should not turn the other cheek. I told Martin Luther King that I could possibly ruin the peaceful thing he wanted to do because I fully believed that in our society there was a faction that did not believe in anything but force and did not have the receptors to receive the peaceful message he was trying to introduce. Besides, I said that in India when people put on passive resistance and would not work, the whole country stopped, while in our country if a handful of blacks decided to strike, some other people would do their jobs. In India the Indians were truly a majority, but in our country the black people were a minority. What we needed was some punishment in our society, where when people were lynched in the South, a group would investigate it and the people who did it would be hanged or shot on their own terms. I thought this would stop a lot of hard-core people who were used to attacking blacks and minority groups without any sort of reprisal.

He shook his head and looked at me sadly and said, "there's one way not to go, and that is the way." And he said to me, "You'll be one of those who will be able to see what will happen by using a peaceful means, and that in this country that it is wholly possible to work within the structure and still achieve, and we will overcome all those people who think that we can do nothing." I said that I would wait and see, but that I thought I wasn't the only one who felt the way I did. We talked about how I had grown up and went to school there, and how I had become an Air Force officer, and other people came up and joined our conversation.

That last year in the Air Force was one in which I spent most of my time doing a thousand odd jobs. General McCauley received another star and was promoted up to Sampson Air Base in Massachusetts, and the next general, General Owes came in. General Owes was a squash man, so the basketball players fell on hard time. I got a job as a visiting officers quarters inspector, supply officer, mess officer, and provost marshal on the base, in a defensive legal posture between the base and the general public. I worked hard. I was on duty almost 24 hours a day. I had difficulty getting my weekends off to play basketball. As Provost Marshal I worked with some interesting cases. There was an idiot on the base who was signing checks, and we caught him. There was an airman who came back drunk and burned himself up as well as a $50,000 barrack. Another airman stole a car, and when the police came up and asked him to turn on his headlights, the airman got into a 100 mile an hour chase and killed himself driving the car into a pole. Another airman took a .45 pistol off base, which was illegal, and got into a wrestling match with some kids at a bar. He ended up shooting himself through the arm and into his own head, killing himself and leaving a brand-new wife and a young baby. All of those cases required that I write a line of conduct letter so their families could receive $10,000 for their deaths. I worked with the FBI on the Weinberger kidnapping, where the child was found dead. The kidnapper was an immigrant who dropped the kid off in a wooded area when he saw a police car, and the child died of exposure. We took samples of signatures from the base and from nearby department stores, and it was one of the charge accounts at a discount store that trapped the kidnapper. After all the work on that case with the FBI, I was still sad to see that immigrant caught up in the trap of easy credit and the fact that his act had cost a small child his life.

I also worked on another sad case of five homosexual girls who got involved with an Indian girl who had been brought up with a whole tribe of brothers and had no interest in female life. We got all of them out of the barracks, and she confessed involvement. I spent time with the girls' psychiatrist, which was interesting but not fruitful. They all received less than honorable discharges. There were multiple episodes of wife beating and drunken fights in nearby bars, as well as court appearances on behalf of Air Force personnel who had gone AWOL or got into fights in nearby communities. We had to keep an eye on the actual Communists in the Long Island area and be responsible for base defense. It was a long and interesting year. I continued to play basketball on weekends; at one time I was play-ing for four different basketball teams, including base teams. My friend Ed Weiner, who told me about Italy, was on the Hazelton team.

After that basketball season, Grace and I were still having our domes-tic difficulties. To get out of the house, I took an extra job as an encyclopedia salesman. I wasn't sure what was going to happen to Grace and the children. As I was thinking about this, the recruiter from Italy came to see me when I was playing an All Star game on Long Island. The coach for the All Star team had coached one of the teams I had beaten, and so he started me in the second quarter so that his own players could have a chance to impress the Italian recruiter. I could have broken that coach's nose, but I just sat there on the bench waiting. There is a rule that there are ten players on an All Star team, and each player gets to play one half. I had to play the second, of course. As it turned out, each time I went into the game, we were about six points or so behind, and I scored a fast ten to put us about four up. I think

I scored 23 points or so, but early in the last quarter I pulled a muscle when I was doing a dunk shot. Ordinarily I would have picked myself up, but I could hardly move, and I saw the whole Italian trip going down the drain. So I stood outside and did not move too much. I shot these long shots, twenty or twenty-five feet, and they hit the rim and bounced in, about four of them. That really broke the game up. We won the game. The recruiter, Mr. Laylo Zombinelli, said he was going to Chicago and then to South America, but he thought I would be his man, and that he would get in contact and work out some kind of a contract with me. I said, "Look, the only thing I really wanted out of basketball, that I never got a chance to get, was to become a doctor." He said that the Italian university would take me into medical school with no problem. "I will go over and straighten the whole thing out and send you back a contract, and tell you what we can pay you, and if we have gotten you into medical school."

After I got out of the Air Force, I felt it might have been a good idea to stay in. I was doing well; I enjoyed my work, and I thought it was important. But having this opportunity to go to Europe and play for Jobert-McGanty and the ball bearing factory gave me a chance to reach out for medicine, something that I feared was slipping by. I was still just as passionate about becoming a doctor as I had been when I was nine years old. I told all my friends that I was going to go to Europe and become a doctor, and the vast majority laughed at me and said, "Johnson the dreamer." And they used to whisper things behind my back, like, "The guy's nuts, leaving pro-basketball to go to Europe and learn Italian." Some people said outright that I was crazy. One of the people that my mother worked for was an executive for Texaco in New York. He said to me frankly, "Johnson, you can't do this. The only people who have been able to go over there and learn a language and come back to this country and be doctors are Jews. It doesn't make sense to waste that kind of time. You ought to play professional basketball and become a good coach." I told him that I was going to try.

I didn't hear from the Italian recruiter for about three months, and then he wrote and said that everything was great. He worked out a salary that was good, and we had to wait to go over to Italy. He asked me to come in June, so that I could learn the language before school started. So I went on practicing basketball every day to get myself ready to go over to Italy and study medicine and play basketball for this Italian team. This was in 1957, and every day I went out to the park to shoot. June came, and the guys asked, "Well, I thought you were going to Italy?" It looked embarrassing because I had not heard from the recruiter for about four weeks or so. Finally, the tickets came. The day we were leaving for Italy, Grace and I had another argument, and I asked her why she didn't stay in the United States, and I would go and find a house and then send for her and the children. Then we would not need to go through so many hectic moments and have more squabbling. I could even go over and stay just for the school year and come back for the summer. Then we could go back the next Fall. She said, "No, I will never let you go by yourself. You will just run off with one of those Italian girls over there." So for that reason she came along, or at least that was the reason she gave me. I was sure she wanted to live in Italy and Europe for a while.

Italy

We had a two-berth cabin on the Julio Cesere. The two children were tiny. They were put into little nets. Chino was about eleven weeks old, and he had to have his diaper changed all the time, as well as bottles. It was a real scene. Grace hardly got out of the cabin to do much of anything. We went out for meals and on deck only once or twice. The trip took eleven days, and it was rough. Our first stop was Naples. We got off the boat, and it was fantastic to see the old piers and buildings, the pastel colors and the great sunlight. What struck me most were the odors and colors and sizes of the vegetables, the garlic hanging, and then the sounds: the high-pitched automobile horns and the rhythmic, melodic musical language the people were speaking, so diametrically different from the guttural sounds of English. That night, back on board, we were invited to the captain's table to dine with him. Apparently he had been listening to the on-shore radio, and I was fast becoming an Italian celebrity. The sportscaster was playing up the fact that I had given up American professional basketball, especially that I had given up a contract with the Harlem Globetrotters, who were world renowned, to pursue the study of medicine in Italy. Because of my arrival, my team was expected to be a favorite for the championship of Italy.

The next day we landed at Genoa. We met the person responsible for my invitation to play and study in Italy. With him had come the entire basketball team in great caravan of cars. At that time, the road from Genoa to Bologna was mountainous and winding. The trip took eight to nine hours. On the way, I had my first encounter with an Italian bathroom. We had stopped at an Italian gas station, and I went to go to the toilet. I looked around for a place to go on the floor. In this room there was slowly running water between two stones that stood like an island. It became obvious to me that I had to get to the two stones and squat down to have a bowel movement. Then there was the search for toilet paper, which turned out to be some old newspaper that was cut into squares and pushed onto a wire coat hanger hung on a nearby wall. That was on the main road between Genoa and Bologna in 1957.

The ride down into Bologna was highlighted by racing around the mountains with horns blasting and races between different cars in our caravan. I noted that a lot of the signs on the road were for American products like Coca Cola, General Electric, US Rubber, Esso, and Texaco. I asked the Italians why there were so many American brands in their market, and their answer was that they had lost the war.

In Bologna, there were a lot of people waiting at the Viatus Country Club, which is the oldest country club in Italy. We arrived at eleven or twelve at night. People were cheering, and some people ran off in different directions with our children because they had never seen black children before. They were friendly, and it was a super meeting. We got an apartment in the good part of town with a fenced garden and a roof top that we could play on that had plants on it. The apartment had a large dining room and a kitchen, two large bedrooms and a bath. The refrigerator was full of Italian food and cold drinks. My contract was great. I had no bills at all, and I got about $600 a month I could bank, which was about the minimum salary that the pro-leaguers were getting in the States, about $7500. I didn't have to pay for electricity, or medical bills, or rent, and we got a round trip to the United States. I had a six-year contract instead of one year, and a maid came in to do heavy washing, while a different maid came in to do light washing and cooking. Every time I scored twenty points or more, I got 10,000 lira, which was enough to live on for a week and what some people made in a month. I was finally getting a chance to study medicine and become a doctor.

There were men in town who had never seen a really beautiful black woman like Grace. They followed her through the streets and waited to see her at the games. She was pampered in every way. She had her own dress maker who made her the finest designs. There were a lot of fabric stores around, so she had every type of material she wanted for dresses. The Italians were used to seeing black men from the soldiers and athletes who came over, but a black woman was, indeed, a welcome oddity. We went yachting and we went to the beach on weekends.

I was taken down to the university the next day and introduced to its director, who was our team doctor and also a professor in the school of medicine. It was determined that while I did not have the required courses to get into the third semester of the sixth year of the medical program in Italy, I could start in the first semester of pre-medical courses. These courses would supplement my degree in social studies and psychology from the

United States and would be adequate for admission to medical school. I had taken the precaution to call Trenton prior to leaving the United States and to ask about my ability to practice medicine in New Jersey after I had finished at the Italian university. I was told that so long as I had an Italian medical degree and passed the foreign medical graduates' examination, then the New Jersey State Boards in Medicine would accept me as a practicing physician. Meanwhile I had an Italian professor who was almost a pal and came daily to teach me Italian before school started in October. I liked the language and learned to communicate with my teammates.

I became a celebrity. I was in the movies, on television and in the magazines and newspapers. Every place I signed autographs. Early in September we had our first tournament. I had eaten some clams and spaghetti, and I thought it was an outstanding dish. I ordered the same dish in Rome, and that night on the boat from Rome to Messina, I became violently ill with tremendous temperatures, sweating and diarrhea. I could not speak Italian well enough at the time, and I was running back and forth all night to the bathroom. The next day we won, but I played poorly, and I continued to have all those symptoms. The next night I was sick as a dog and I stayed in the house away from everyone. In that series of games we played France, Czechoslovakia, and other Italian teams as well as an English team. We won the tournament, but I continued to be terribly sick, and at the end of the ten-day tour in Sicily, I had lost twenty-two pounds. When I came back, the team doctor put me in bed, where I stayed for eight or nine days. Apparently I had caught typhoid without knowing it. I regained my strength, but I didn't regain the weight that first year.

It was suddenly October and time to go to the university to start pharmacy school and then medical school. One day I saw Peter Pierotti, the person who had lived on Armory Street across from me, whose father and uncle had a tremendous fist fight with Mr. Slivey. I hadn't seen him for a good many years. He asked me what I was doing there, and I told him I was there playing basketball and starting medical school.

Over the summer, my father in the United States had gone into Mr. Pierotti's tailoring shop. He was extremely prejudiced, though he got on with my father. My father had gone to see him just to tell him about me, because he knew Mr. Pierotti's son was in Italy studying medicine and was going to become a doctor in Italy, and my father wanted to brag about his son who was going to become a doctor in Italy, too. It turned out that his son Peter had received a letter from his father, and he looked me up and said he had been reading about me in the papers over the summer, though he was not sure I was the same guy from his street. He asked me about me premed work, and I said I had not taken any, but that I was going into the first semester of medical school. He appeared upset and said he had had a tough time as an Italian fighting all the Irish students to get into medical school. He said I probably needed to go back and go through what he had to get into med school. I told him I had written Trenton and they said that so long as I came with a degree and passed the examinations, they would accept me.

When it came time to register, Peter volunteered to come with me and translate, because my Italian was not that good. So he went along and talked to the people in the admissions office, and before I knew it I was in pharmacy, and the director said that unless I went back to the U.S. and took pre-med courses, I would never be able to transfer, and the only thing they could offer me was a degree in pharmacy. I felt that someone had pulled a rug out from underneath me. I felt terribly deceived. Not only could I not fulfill my dream, I had a wife who and two children, and my wife was becoming increasingly unhappy and enormously upset for having taken the children out of the U.S. on a promise that I could study medicine. I could have played basketball in the United States, but it was now October, and the teams had been selected, so I had no choice but to stay. Peter intervened and went to the people who had written my contract and got it changed so I was paid double my salary, due to the fact that I could not study medicine, only pharmacy. I thought I could become a pharmacist in the U.S. by passing exams. I was sick most of that year. A heavy fog settles on Bologna about November that comes and goes through March. It becomes very cold for about a week and then goes right into a very hot summer.

Because I was sick, we lost the Italian championship by one point. I did not have any trouble renewing my contract for the next year. On the family level, Grace and I were fighting more and more. She was obviously flattered by having Italian men follow her everywhere. I thought she was making me pay for the letter to Gretchen. There were times when she would not come to bed or she would put me out of bed and tell me to go out on the streets to chase down other women if that was all I wanted to do. Our sexual thing became a huge problem, and we fought most of the time about that. I was in an awkward position. I was the only black in town, and if I went out to buy a newspaper, it was written up in the paper. I was very Catholic and was a friend of the local Cardinal. That first Easter, my baby Chino was chosen as a mascot of Italy for their Baby Day Parade. Anything I did was talked about or written about, so in short Grace made me pay for what had happened in the United States. I studied hard to pass my pharmacy courses.

When the academic year ended, I was preparing for exams in physics, geology and anatomy, and Peter Pierotti showed up at our house in a state of dire anxiety. He said he had failed his medicine and surgery exams and needed to pass them to graduate from medical school. In Italy you can take a program for eight years, and there is no particular limit on the number of times you can take an examination. If you failed in both medicine and surgery, you could not graduate. For Peter, that was especially dramatic, because he had already sold his apartment and his furniture, and he had married an Italian girl. He also had his tickets to go back to America with his new wife. He could not afford to look for a place and settle down for another six months, which is what it usually took to retake those examinations. Peter came to me because I knew one of the professors in the medical department. He asked me to go over and ask for the right to take the exam again without waiting six months. I called the professor and told him that I had made arrangements for a going away party for my friend Peter, who had studied medicine in Bologna. The professor came over and talked to Peter, and they made arrangements for Peter to take the exam over again in his office. He went over, and allegedly he retook and passed the exam. Eventually he was a surgeon at the Englewood Hospital.

The professor came over to our basketball practice about a week later and called me aside. He said he couldn't understand my purpose in helping out Peter. I asked him what he meant. He asked if I didn't know that Peter had told the medical school that I should not be allowed into medicine until I went back to the United States and took the proper courses to be admitted. Then the admissions officer and the director decided that I would not be allowed to study medicine unless I took American pre-med, despite the fact that they had previously agreed to accept me into the school. I told the professor that I did not understand Italian well at that time, so I did not know what Peter had done out of his continuing prejudice. I never told Peter that I found out. He did arrange for me to get a better financial contract.

My second year started out a lot stronger. I put back the weight I had lost. I could speak Italian better and the other team members were trusting me a bit more. We played a lot better basketball. However, in the middle of the year the Italian Olympic Committee decided that foreign basketball players would no longer be able to play in the leagues as preparation for the Olympics. Now only Italians could play to get ready for the 1960 Olympics. This was the '58-'59 season. I had a six-year contract, and I was actively going to the university. I decided that the owners would have to honor my contract or pay me the additional four years in some kind of settlement. When that year ended, we lost the championship again to the same team, by one point. My team stopped paying me, and I had no other way to earn money in Italy. I would have needed a work permit to do anything else, and the Italians did not issue many of those then. So there I sat with no income, two children and a wife in a country in which I could not work. I was a friend of the Cardinal in town, which was the only thing that saved me. I went to him and I wrote to the Pope in Rome, and he got his secretary of sports to write to me and to the Olympic team, saying they would have to take care of me in some way. The owner of the team was a stockbroker for all the grain in Italy and he owned grain elevators as well. He elected to pay half my salary and make sure I had enough to eat while the team organization fought the Olympic Committee, since it was that committee that had decided that foreigners could no longer play in the country.

I was sweating out the whole thing. Every day I went to the team office to find out if anything was being done. I had a good legal case to collect the four years of salary, but if the case went to court, it might take eight to ten years to settle in the Italian legal system. What was I supposed to do for those eight years? I worked out every day and tried to stay in shape. I traveled with the team as a manager and ball boy, after being the star of the team. On one such occasion we were playing in a summer tournament against a Swiss team. One of the players on the team, a guy named Phillip, spoke English. He walked up to me and said, "What are you doing, just tossing out balls and helping coach the team? Don't you play anymore?"

I explained the new rule in Italy but also how the Italians were thinking of building a team around me in Bolgona. Then he asked me why I had come to Italy, and I explained about medical school and pharmacy school. Phillip said, "Listen, come to Geneva, Switzerland. There is an excellent medical school there that is recognized by the U.S. You will have no problem getting into school. You can play for our basketball team and pay for some of your schooling, but we cannot give you the kind of contract you had from the Italians." The team offered to pay for my trip up to Geneva if I would play for them. They also arranged for a studio for me until I found an apartment. I went back home and told Grace that I had another shot at medical school. She was upset that I was not going to take her and the two children up to Switzerland, but we didn't have the money, and I didn't want to ask the team to pay for tickets for three more people. So she stayed in Bologna and I went to Switzerland.

The train ride up was exciting. Switzerland was far cleaner. I played well for them. Their level of play was lower than Italy's. The owner of the team took me to the admissions office at the university. I had brought along transcripts and letters of recommendation. The admissions officer said that I had done a good job in pharmacy, but that they would not accept any Italian or American credits. If I wanted to get into pre-med school, they would allow me one chance to make it. If I failed any subject, they would expel me, and I would not be given a second chance. He also said that if I was willing to start from scratch, they would waive the six-month period for learning French, which most people had to take for the examinations. Since

I already spoke Italian, one of their national languages, they would allow me to enter without French. I took the train back to Bologna. On the train I became frightened. Here I was, 28 years old. I had a possible chance to open a basketball school back in the United States; I possibly had four years of salary coming to me. I was not sure I could cut the mustard in pre-med classes in Geneva. And then there was the question of French and moving three people and participating in the raising of my children. I thought maybe I should leave well enough alone. I couldn't sleep. It kept coming back to me that this was my opportunity, my chance. If God meant for me to become a doctor, now was the time for me to try all I could to fulfill that dream. When I got back to Italy, I spoke to Grace and told her that I had been accepted and that I would like to take this chance to go to medical school in Geneva. She said, "Are you sure that this is what you want?" She was upset because I had suggested that she take the children and go home to New Jersey and live in my mother's house, and I would come home each summer. We were not getting along that well anyway, and in the summers I could work to have enough money to come back to Geneva for school. I had enough money in the bank to send Grace and the children home. She said, "No." She did not want to go home, and she did not want to leave me in Italy or Switzerland alone, because she thought I would run off with some white lady. She liked living in Europe better than living in the U.S.

Thinking over my contract, I knew that I wanted to play, not just coach. So I asked the Italian team to pay me for one year rather than four and release me. They agreed, and we left for Switzerland. On that train to Geneva, Grace and I had a lively conversation about her going back to the United States. She had not worked for over two years. She had stayed home in delightful luxury with maids doing her housework and often helping with the cooking. She had many trips to the beach and the mountains, as well as all the clothes she wanted, with men following her from store to store. She wasn't enthusiastic about having to go back to work eight hours a day. When the train got to Milano, I was preoccupied, and I left my briefcase on the train with all my publicity notices and $8000. When I remembered it, I went racing back, leaping over tracks and back to the other train. Just as I got to the compartment door, one of the railroad employees was leafing through the briefcase and starting to count the money. I yelled, "Hold it. That's my briefcase and that is my money." He would not give me the briefcase, and he called the police and the railroad officials. He was screaming that he had found the briefcase and should be allowed to keep it. Despite my pictures in the briefcase and the fact that I had come right back for it, I had to pay $800 to the head of the railroad station to get the case back, as well as sign an untold number of papers. So the railroad attendant got 10% of what he had found. The only reason they gave me the rest was the publicity pictures of me. That was the last kick in the face from Italy, which at least had got me to Europe and into pharmacy school, which was a scientific course of study. I had also learned Italian, though an Italian-American had kept me out of medical school.

Switzerland and Medical School

Switzerland was beautiful, cultivated up to the mountaintops. Unlike Italy, there were no signs of World War Two, such as damaged buildings with gaping holes in their walls. At first the Swiss were more distant and aloof. The people left you alone. They were very precise, like their watches. There were more blacks around who were involved with the United Nations, so we were not such oddities. We moved into a little studio near the English church. The studio was a large room in an attic that had been beautifully re-painted in light pastel colors. The only drawback was that the bathroom was out in the hall, and three other studios shared it with us. We did have a wash basin in our room. We started to look around for another apartment very soon, not because of the noise of the bathroom or sharing it with other studios. People were walking and running in the hall at all hours. One night, after visiting some friends, we came back and saw two ladies standing inside the hall dressed for hire. I can remember the look on Grace's face when she figured out what was going on. There was a flourishing prostitution business in town and in our own house. We found another place a couple of blocks from the United Nations offices. A black guy named Benny sold us the apartment for about $2000. It was on the fifth floor in a clean building with a balcony that overlooked a large play area the size of three or four ball fields. From the balcony in the spring we could see huge rainbows, and I felt as if I had come to the bottom of a rainbow where I could find the golden happiness I had been searching for.

Grace took about three months to find a job. She found work in a Catholic organization that helped Hungarian refugees and rapidly became the assistant to the rector of the organization because she could speak Italian and English rapidly and could get along in French. She liked to spend her money on clothes. In the interim we struggled along on the money we had saved from the basketball years in Italy and from the salary the local team paid me. I devoted myself to learning French and trying to study medicine. I was finally having the opportunity to go to medical school after chasing it since the age of nine. I studied every minute that I was not eating, sleeping or playing basketball, which paid the rent. I was a hermit, dribbling a ball to my court or to my bedroom, sometimes staying up twenty hours a day. I can remember getting pins and needles in my butt from not moving from one spot to another for hours on end. I lived on orange juice and vitamins. I was not easy to get along with. Each day consisted of going to classes and listening hard to the French so that I did not miss anything. I went to every class there was. I did not take French lessons. I just translated my French textbooks to English and picked up French as I played with the team and worked with my Swiss lab partners. A friend named Portman gave me his French class notes, which I translated into English and returned each morning. Then I would read ahead, so that I knew what the lecturer was likely to be talking about the next day. I struggled.

I played basketball with the same team I had joined, which was in about sixth place when I arrived. I was probably in the best shape I had ever been: 220 pounds and 6'5." Every morning in Italy I had run three or four miles and jumped rope. I used my conditioning to bring that team from sixth place to first in the Swiss industrial and regular basketball leagues. We won the Swiss cup. I played on the university's team, and we won the national university basketball championship. All that induced students to help me, though the professors did not like the mix of sports and study.

Grace and I had a hard time. She was a good person, but we were in competition over who had the more important job, and she was angry that I lived like a hermit, didn't go out, and didn't do much with the children. The year ended well for basketball and for academics. I didn't have to take any exams, though there was a block of exams I had to take within three semesters to proceed. At the age of 29, I felt I had no time to delay, and though I was not prepared in French, I could explain atomic structure, anatomy, general chemistry or biology. What I could not do was ask for bread or go to the store and buy clothes. Once you presented for this exam, you could not take it again for six months. Generally, you were given two chances, but I had been told that I would have only one chance to pass. If I failed, I would be dismissed from the school. The exams there were different. They were all oral except for one chemistry exam that was based on the experiments we did in lab. The oral exam covered comparative anatomy, chemistry, organic and inorganic chemistry, genetics, general and medical botany, experimental physics, and zoology.

The exams took place over a period of about two weeks. You were ushered into a large amphitheater and sat in the stands. The general public was invited, and a lot of relatives from foreign countries came, especially from Arabia, Greece and Italy. The exams started at eight in the morning. On the floor of the amphitheater the professor sat at a table with a visiting professor from another university and an assistant. Your name was called. They would say, "Johnson," and then you went down the stairs to a long table and took one of the cards placed face down on the table and flipped it over. You were given about fifteen minutes to discuss your question. I can still remember my first question, which was: Explain the evolution of the uro-genital system from frogs to man and talk about sex-linked hereditary problems and genetics. And then you talked. You opened your mouth and you talked for ten or fifteen minutes for each subject. Then the professors would discuss your answer among themselves, right there on the spot in front of the public audience, and tell you immediately if you passed and could go on to the next series of examinations. It was a horror show. My French was not good, but I could talk on the subjects. I passed that whole battery of examinations over a two-week period, and then I went wild. I knew that I still had five years to go, but I felt like I could make it with the help of God. That year 68% of the students who presented failed. I was the only American who had presented who passed.

I recognized then that Grace's attitude was being conveyed to my two children. I was not spending enough time with the family. I was not being a good father. She impressed upon me that I had taken time from the family and that I could study less and spend more time with them. My French improved. We began to go out to eat occasionally and to movies. Grace got better jobs, and she hired a maid who helped at home, Wherever she worked, she usually ended up as the president's or vice-president's secretary, though she often fought with other staff. She came to speak fluent French. She was highly intellectual, but our relationship was always precarious and capricious. After working for the Hungarian refugees, she went to American Machine and then to the Organization of Petroleum Exporting Countries (OPEC), which was Saudi Arabia, Kuwait and so on. She was reasonably happy there. OPEC threw many parties, and she was generally the hostess of these catered affairs, in addition to directing their many conferences. We argued about her desire to travel to other countries and cities to participate in these meetings. I still thought she did not support me in my desire to become a doctor and that she spent too much of her money on clothes to keep up her appearance for these jobs as executive secretary. Sometimes she bought more clothes when I needed books. She held the purse strings on what she earned. As a result, I felt emasculated. She told friends that I was a terrible father, that I didn't spend any time with the children, and that I spent all my time studying or on the basketball court. Yet we did go to many picnics in France, to the French coast, to the Riviera and once to a castle in Spain for a month. We did many things an average American family could not dream of doing

I borrowed ten thousand dollars from the New York State Loan Society and also borrowed from my father and brothers to help me pay my own bills. I continued to spend most of my time studying for exams, and my basketball suffered because I did not go to practice as much. That second year we won the university basketball championship and the Swiss cup, but we did not win the national independent league championship. The people on the team were very unhappy with me. As a result, I moved to a different team with some more American players. Now that I was in the third semester, I joined a group of students who had done pre-med in America. They had been officially admitted to the school of medicine, while I was considered in the school of science until I completed that term. A lot of those Americans wanted nothing to do with me, because I was not officially in the medical school. They talked down to me, though that was difficult, as I was 6'5." Many of them were prejudiced. They talked as well about their American academic records and how they felt mistreated because they had not been accepted to medical school in the United States.

As time went on these Americans found that I had loads of Swiss friends and no need to follow them around, join their American club, or borrow money from them. When they found that I had no need for them, they started to come around, especially when exam time came. At the end of the sixth semester, the Americans wanted to get into study groups with the Swiss to make sure their pronunciation and their presentations in French would be acceptable to the professors. It was a complete turnaround for many of them. One of the guys I studied with decided that he would not present for the exams. At that point we had to take a series of exams that focused on physiology, histology, embryology, anatomy and biochemistry. In the first part we had to go to the labs and do experiments like dissections of frogs' legs, blood typing, and calculations in biochemistry. We also did the dissection of an arm or leg and microscopic studies for histology and embryology. If you passed that, you came back for the theoretical portion, where you explained the dissection of a brain or heart, or you explained about hemostasis or other phenomena. About 57% failed this the first time around. I was the only American going in the first time who passed. The friend I studied with went back to Englewood, New Jersey to do an externship. At Englewood, he met Peter Pierotti, who was responsible for my not getting into medical school in Italy. My friend told Peter that I was in medical school and passing my exams, and Peter almost flipped out. He could not believe that I had gotten into medical school and that I was doing all right. Peter didn't say what he had done; he sent back his best regards and said he would help me when I got back to the States. I felt no need to say anything, because it was to my advantage to know exactly what kind of person he was and how he had cost me two and a half years of my life.

I passed that set of examinations with grades high enough that the professor of anatomy asked me to act as instructor in his dissection lab, which I did for three semesters. By then I had become quite proficient in French. Because I had no money to go away in the summers, I spent that time working in the hospital learning things that one does not ordinarily learn in a European medical school. I also worked at the United Nations for two months of one four-month vacation. I enjoyed working for the U.S. delegation to the U.N. I ran secret messages back and forth to the U.S. mission, I mimeographed secret papers at night, and worked a teletype machine from Secretary of State Dean Rusk's office to the Geneva delegation. I interpreted on occasion, using my French and Italian, and got to meet people like James Roosevelt and Adlai Stevenson. When I met Stevenson he asked me to tell my story, and he gave me a signed copy of his last address to the U.N. just a few days before he died in London of a heart attack.

As for basketball, during the six years I was in Switzerland, we won five out of six university titles, ten Geneva cups, and one national tournament. Between working as an instructor, and for the UN, and borrowing money from my parents and the New York educational fund, and playing basketball, I worked my way through medical school. We had many fine things that were due to Grace's work. She had an Austin, and I had a Peugeot 404. The children went to a fine school. Grace traveled with me to European games. I went to Czechoslovakia, France, Spain and Belgium, and even one year played against the American Olympic team that included Oscar Robinson, Ralph Bellamy, Jerry West, and Jerry Lucas. Of course we lost to them, by about fifty points, but I still have an emblem from the Olympic team that Oscar Robinson gave to me.

I also played against Russian teams, as well as teams from Bulgaria, Albania, Poland and Romania. When we arrived in Europe, Hungary had just had its revolution, and while we were there the Algerian war went on, so that any time we went to France, I would be searched because of my black skin and ostracized as an African until they found out I was an American. We were in Belgium when the Congo was taken over by the blacks. While this made me more aware of the stupidity of American racism, though I thought we were working it out, I also noticed that Switzerland imported Italian, French and Spanish people for the tourist season and then shipped them out when they were not needed. Those workers are not able to stay or to move around, and they are discriminated against while they are in Switzerland. I also found that blacks from Africa who came to Switzerland discriminated against me because most of them were princes or from rich families, and they never needed to work hard at the universities because of their names. Their grandparents had not been slaves. Moreover, I realized when I went to the Communist bloc that there were even young people, fourteen years of age, who were not allowed to go out of their family housing or meet more than one or two people at a time. Or if they were athletes or artists, they could not take family members with them out of their countries. I had one friend from Czechoslovakia who wanted to be a doctor, but the country needed engineers, so that was what he had to study. His nation's needs took precedence over what he wanted as an individual. I saw how the gypsies were treated, too, and I decided that my own country is closer than any other to a Utopia. The poorest American can be richer than the average person in a country like Spain or Portugal, for example. Nowhere I went did I see the majority giving in to the minority. There were no helping hands, only slaps. And there were no such things as the athletic scholarships that I and my brothers had used to achieve our educations. One of my professors in Switzerland said that blacks should not be doctors, they should be clergy. It sent shivers up my spine to think this man was going to give me an examination, but by the time I came up he was sick, and we later found out he was a morphine addict. Before I graduated, he died of an overdose. The European experience netted me a doctor of medicine and a master of science and a wealth of scientific knowledge. However, the most important thing it gave me was a strengthening of my self-worth, self-respect and dignity that my father had pushed me to get.

The next year of medical school I got into clinical medicine. I enjoyed taking care of people and being with them. I thought at first that I might want to get into psychiatry. In one of my first externship appointments I was working in Dr. Mack's service, which was an honor service, even though when you had it, you did absolute coolie work in the whole hospital. Professor Mack had a great reputation in therapeutic medicine. He had an American doctor working with him at that time named Lenny Bernstein. I already had this degree in social studies and psychology from Duquesne, and I thought that once I finally got into medical school, I would take advantage of both degrees by getting into psychiatry.

There was an interesting law in Switzerland where during the first 48 hours before anyone is committed to a mental institute, they had to be observed in a hospital ward, and all medical possibilities causing their comportment had to be investigated. Because I had expressed an interest in psychiatry, an aide told me to examine all the patients who were coming in for the wait before being committed to Belair, the mental institution. On one occasion I had this very young Italian girl who was married to a Swiss man and living in Switzerland. She had what is commonly called post-partum psychosis. She had tried to kill a little baby by throwing the baby from an attic window. She was caught just in time to prevent her from killing the baby, and she presented a special problem. In the French and German speaking parts of Switzerland the Italians are discriminated against in much the same manner as the American black is in the United States. Certain housing is denied. Certain hotels do not have them as their guests. The people in the streets degrade them, and they are given the most menial types of jobs. If they are not citizens, they are imported for tourist season and then expelled. They are also not allowed to bring in their families if they are not Swiss citizens. That is why Switzerland has no unemployment; people are shuttled in and out as they are needed. This Italian lady had come as a maid and fallen in love with one of the members of the household. They had married, but when her child was born she verbalized how horrible it was to be Italian in the surrounding French speaking areas. She said she did not wish her child to suffer as she had suffered at the hands of her employers. So she elected to kill her child. She kept re-living this incident, when she went to the window sill and had the child ready to be shoveled out the window and her husband stopped her. Each day I came in and talked to her about how she could make it and help her child have a good life, and how she could teach her child to love and respect himself so that he could withstand the pressures of prejudice and discrimination and segregation. I poured myself out to her. If I saw her in the morning, she would understand and that afternoon she would be all right. Then the next morning she would slip back and not understand and not want to understand and say the child would be better off dead. I kept treading over the same ground with her and never made any headway. I felt drained as if I had played three or four basketball games. I had mental fatigue, and I kept going back to ground zero. So I felt that I would not follow up on psychiatry. After this frustrating experience, I looked for a specialty in medicine that I would be at home with and that would be more fulfilling and more suited to my personality. I decided that surgery was a dynamic, do-something-about-it discipline. The rest of my time at Geneva, I became the vice president of the medical school student body, and I became the first American to win the monetary award for athletic and academic excellence.

I have many fond memories of the professors at the university, their spirit, the atmosphere and the girls there, and the realization that I had a lot of friends in the medical school, the student body, and among the physicians, politicians and sports people I had known in those years in Europe. I felt sad to leave the beautiful city of Geneva where I was an appreciated and functioning member of society, but I felt an urgency to return to the United States. I returned to the U.S. in December 1965.

An American Physician

It was a tremendous cultural shock to arrive at Kennedy International Airport. It had been eight and a half years since I had been in the United States. One of my first impressions was the filth on the streets of New York. Like the Swiss, I had come to understand that filth on streets did not blow there. It had to be placed there by individuals whose personal habits did not provide them with enough pride to carry trash and other debris to a public trashcan. Next was the noise, the blowing of horns and the loud conversations. It was another world after our adventure in Switzerland. This was also the summer of burn, baby, burn. There were riots going on, racial in their intent. At first, I had little concern with that, because I had to find a place to work and to have my internship and then go on to residency, if that is what I decided to do. I went down to Bellevue Hospital looking for an internship, and I was dismayed at the disorderly and ineffective hospital scene I encountered there. Its physical plan was outrageously large. Geneva Hospital had one thousand beds, but the facilities were more modern than nine out of ten hospitals in the U.S. I was appalled, just looking at Bellevue. Everything looked helter-skelter. I went to Columbia Hospital. These hospitals were recommended to me by prominent professors in Europe, and I did not expect there would be any trouble getting an internship, but I was disappointed at the attitude of the individuals I encountered, who were condescending. I hesitated to go to any more city hospitals to look at their internship programs and decided to go to a small community hospital in Englewood, New Jersey, for an internship.

One day I went out with my brother David, who had become a detective, to see how he worked in the field. He told me stories about what was going on in the south Bronx. One of the secretaries in his office told me about the Montefiore Hospital, where she said there was a lot of personal attention given to patients and where the building was not a 50 or 60 story structure with beds seemingly piled one on top of another. I went over just to look at it. There was some grass around the building and flowers out front. There were some houses in the neighborhood, and the hospital itself had 800 to 900 beds. The complex was spread over five or six blocks, and the grounds were nicely kept. I went in and met an administrator who told me what they were doing there and how they were one of the more progressive hospitals in the city, if not the nation. We toured and looked at the wards and talked to people on the floors, both nurses and the house staff, and I felt I could grow in that situation. The people I met were impressed by the obstacles I had overcome to become an M.D., and they said I probably had a good chance to get into their program. I matched them well on their internship matching program. The only drawback was that I could not start that January; I would have to start July first. I hated to waste six months, but this was a good residency internship, and I would be the first foreign graduate they would be taking. So I went back to Englewood to talk to the hospital there about working for just six months.

At Englewood I had to learn to speak English, because everything I had done in medicine was in French. For those six months my pronunciation was a combination of English, French and Italian. Englewood also gave me a chance to show that a black intern could work out in a hospital that served a majority affluent white community. Every time there was something to do, I volunteered, and that helped me to learn how to do all the tasks that interns must do, such as starting blood, drawing blood, and putting in Foleys and catheters and things of that nature that we did not do in Europe. Europe was still in that phase of medical teaching in which the professor does the work and the student watches, while in the U.S. medical students start doing the hands-on work even before they know what they are doing. European schools stress the theory of medicine, and only in the internship and residency do the practical skills become a focus.

With a great deal of difficulty, Grace and I stayed together through the internship. She thought I was being a fool by going back to the hospital at all hours to do things and to accept chores and help others out. When we first came back, we had nowhere to live, so me moved in with my mother and father. I thought it would be a good idea to live there for six months and then find a house in the city near the hospital where I interned. That way I could see the children. About once every two months, Grace got into tremendous arguments with my father about one thing or another, whether it was about getting a ride or help with shopping or something else that should have been benign. He asked me to find a house as soon as possible and to leave his. We got out and found an apartment near Teaneck, which kept me running back and forth to the Englewood Hospital. That was unpleasant, but it was probably better for us to be in our own place.

The internship at Englewood allowed me to establish a working relationship with the staff. They invited me to come back and help them in their emergency room during my first months at Montefiore. On my nights off from Montefiore, I usually worked for six hours at Englewood and then went home and slept for six hours before returning to Montefiore for a 36 hour shift. By the time I started my internship at Montefiore, my time at Englewood had taught me everything that American medical graduates could do and then some, because the European theoretical training was better, especially in dermatology, otolaryngology, and ophthalmology. I was usually the first or very close to the first intern to make the diagnosis on a new patient. The next year I applied for a surgical residency and was accepted. Montefiore then decided it would accept two to four foreign graduates each year because of what I had shown them about the training, especially in Switzerland. I made time to take and pass the New York, New Jersey and Pennsylvania boards for state licenses.

No matter how much money I made, it was never enough. Once I was working at Nyack and Englewood as well, we had enough, and then Grace started to feel that we should buy a new house. Yet each time I would take on an extra hospital to provide for her, she would complain that I was out of the house and a poor father. So I always felt inadequate. I spent most of my waking and sleeping hours at the hospitals. I thought I was a great guy, but things just went from bad to worse.

This was the summer of burn, baby, burn. In Englewood and many other communities. In Newark, Cleveland, Chicago and other cities blacks were destroying the ghettos by burning down their own dwellings, their own homes. Living outside the United States I had come to realize that this was probably the greatest country on Earth and that because of all its riches and advances compared to the rest of the world in technology and the medical professions, there would probably always be someone throwing stones and rocks at the U.S. and trying to find her Achilles heel. I remembered my friend in Czechoslovakia, who had not been allowed to study medicine. I remembered the barbed wire and machine guns at the Czech border, the women servicing the trains, the police in the train station with tommie guns, and the mediocre hotel where our basketball team was put up. The people did not seem to have any gaiety about them at all. The streets were poor, and the stores were lacking in variety. I learned that the people who staffed the stores were only allowed to work so many hours per week, so that there were lots of shifts, so that many employees could get part of the action.

On that same trip, after their team beat ours fair and square by six points, we decided we wanted to see their nightclubs and a strip tease joint. We stopped a guy in the street and asked him where we could find a strip club. He didn't speak any French or English. One member of our team spoke fluent German, and as much as the Czechs hated Germans, they still knew the language. The square where we stood had posters that must have been twelve or even twenty feet tall showing Russian tanks liberating the town from Germans. In 1960 those posters were still on display to remind the Czechs that the Russians were their saviors. The man we stopped gave us instructions, and as we left him to go find the place, we looked back and saw this guy accosted by two plainclothes policemen and hurried off. We went into the nightclub. There was no strip tease. They played Dixieland music for us, and a lady sang who was completely clothed. The next day we were asked to leave the hotel, so we left. I returned two years later and things were a bit better for the Czechs. People were impressed that as a black person I didn't have anything tremendously bad to say about the United States. They expressed prejudice against the Gypsies. As for Italy, from what I saw, if you were born a shoemaker's son you would live and die a shoemaker and had no chance to move up in society. There was a small middle class and a small, very wealthy aristocratic class that ruled everything. All the inequities and injustices that I saw in other countries did not show me that America was bad. America might in fact be on the vanguard of racial relationships and social and economic mobility. Democracy means rule by the majority, and that has nothing to do with justice or what is right or wrong. The majority rules, but the minority does not have to sit content with what is going on. In America you can go out and work three, four, five or ten times harder to get somewhere on the educational level. An individual can work for himself and prove that life is worth living. An individual can cope with a society that is racist, segregationist, and discriminatory. Your own self-improvement can help society.

I thought, in that summer of 1965–66, that one of the major problems was that American blacks had not learned that they should really go all out to make themselves better. They should make demands from society, but not in a violent and destructive manner. They should cope by really working nine or ten times harder. The garbageman should tell himself to prepare his child to be a professional man, because that is attainable in this country. A garbageman's son in Italy or Switzerland would remain a garbageman. No other place provided the kind of athletic scholarships like those in America. Here if you pay the price, you have a chance to make it. If you work like hell, your sons and daughters have a chance to make it. The most important thing in life is to love and respect yourself. I do not need to make excuses for my skin color. I do not need the permission of society. I do not need to reach out and say gimme, gimme, because I can do something. I can be a better shoe-shine boy, or a better dishwasher, or a better teacher, or a better doctor or a better businessman. I can do. The only way a black should use his hatred is to drive him to do better. One of the things that I learned to do at school in Geneva was to read one more page for that cracker in Georgia, read one more page for that Southern white, to improve myself and to utilize that hate to be better off.

I felt in the summer of 1966 that too many of my brethren were running and burning their homes without knowing where new homes would come from and without knowing if their families would live through the onslaughts of vicious policemen coming in and trying to put down black uprisings. The blacks had no way to defend themselves. They had no factories. They had no money. They had nothing but loud verbal mouths that were on the verge of destroying many more blacks in ghetto areas. My attitude was that blacks were always too small in number, but they had the ability to improve themselves despite all the attempts by society to keep them in their slave position in society. But there were two million blacks who succumbed to propaganda and who allowed themselves to think of nothing but welfare and not working. They thought that because they were black they could do nothing and just enjoy themselves. In 1954, the separate but equal education standard was turned around by the Supreme Court and blacks had a chance to go forth and get educations. In 1965 those people who tried were now ready for employment. America was forced by public opinion to find places for these educated blacks. A lot of them were put in windows, where they could show others that blacks could do a good job. What this meant for the great number of blacks in the ghetto was that a person who was black could succeed in this society, leave the ghetto, buy a nice house and clothes and cars, and function as affluent blacks on a level with the affluent white society. These blacks went out of the ghetto and bought houses where they were not supposed to buy them. They went to schools where they were not supposed to go and to restaurants where they never ate before. Then suddenly the black who was poor and who was poorly instructed and who had remained in the ghetto could see his black brother outside the ghetto obtain the goals he had set for himself. However, blacks who succeeded were consumed by becoming better and did not reach back into the ghetto in significant numbers to help their brothers. Those who remained in the ghetto could no longer say that blacks could not succeed in this country. There in front of him were shining examples to show him that he could, if he worked hard, succeed. Now he was left in the ghetto and faced with the stark reality that he did not try and was, perhaps, inferior to the man who had left and made it. Those thoughts, I believe, disturbed many ghetto dwellers more than just being in the ghetto.

If all the blacks had stayed in the ghetto, there probably would not have been, in my estimation, the rioting that did go on. What drove the rioting was the attitude that while another black can get out, I am stuck, and what can I do now? The rationalization was that something unfair must have happened that explained why the other black got out. He must have had some help. The only recourse with that frame of mind was to say that you have to be given something to get out. The attitude is that it is the government's job to build better homes than the ones we burn down. From my perspective, the alternative is to take all the people without jobs and get them to go from house to house, reconstructing them inside to outside, one house a month until the ghetto is cleaned up. Take the dirt in the streets that people put there and clean it up. People can help themselves while still protesting inequities and injustices. When I looked back at some of these areas such as Englewood and Washington, D.C. in 1973, seven years later, they still had not been rebuilt.

The verbal loudmouths were the ones that started the hostility and the rioting and everything else that followed in 1966, under the guise of Black is Beautiful and I am Proud to be Black. The people who worked hard believed this anyway; they did not have to wear their hair African style or wear shirts that said, "Black is Beautiful." To swim upstream, you had to believe you were better than the white man. That was something you had to do alone. It was a personal commitment to themselves that they would have to prove on a daily basis and not be deterred by American white society that believed that all blacks are inferior or second-class citizens. I remembered again in school how the girls would not go out with me because they preferred people with lighter skins. There was a whole thing about being a light-skinned black that went back to the time of slavery. This penetrated into society so that black professional people were chosen if they were light or if they had a West Indian accent. Other minority groups did the same. German Jews who came to America thought they were better than Polish Jews. When I encountered African blacks in Switzerland, they would not speak to me. In their countries they were Number One; they had never been slaves, and therefore they were a thousand times better than any American black. When they learned that I was vice president of the student body and an anatomy instructor, they would condescend to me and come and talk about African dress and culture, but I did not give a damn about having an Afro or any of that. My main point is that we must function in the society in which we are born and with the cards that have been dealt to us. I tried to say these things in 1966, but my brothers fought with me and said you will be attacked if you tell these people not to spend so much time on violence and cool themselves down.

That summer I decided that I would go talk at universities and high schools about athletic scholarships and becoming goal oriented, so that you can use that scholarship not just to become a professional athlete but to study law and medicine and teaching. I also talked about V.D. and drug addiction, and I felt that was my contribution to helping blacks. I also made up my mind to be the best cardio-thoracic surgeon I could become. That summer I worked a lot in emergency rooms. I needed the money and it was good for my training. I remember one emergency room in the South Bronx where they saw about a quarter of a million people a year. My most vivid recollection was the many blacks who came in after being stabbed and cut up on the face and not caring about it. They were anxious only to get up from the table, flee harm, and go injure another human being. One Sunday the ambulance brought in a common law couple who had bled to death on their kitchen floor after having raised knives against each other and cut each other all over their faces and chests and arms. All a neighbor could tell us was that it was about some fried fish. The night before he had heard them arguing about fish, and the next morning the neighbor had seen blood dripping from underneath their kitchen door. Events like that painted in my mind that there was a disregard for life itself. This precious thing that God had given to each and every one of us was held in total disrespect. My feeling in essence was that these people had never learned to love themselves. They had never learned to respect themselves. They felt inferior despite the Loud Noise, the Black is Beautiful, and all the violence. They were hurt to the point that they would react violently.

After all my travels I could say that with our telstar objective lens we could visit many lands and the honest among us would have to admit that America is at the Avant-Garde of truly meaningful race relations because of what has already been accomplished with large numbers of the various races that have learned to live in relative peace and harmony. It is one of the miracles of our times.

When I could not find work in emergency rooms, I did house to house calls for the Brown Levy group in Brooklyn. I felt that being black, I had a commitment and an obligation to do something for fellow blacks. I started working there in the wintertime. It was a cold winter with a lot of flu cases, and I was fairly busy. One night I was called out to go see a lady somewhere in the Bronx. She lived in a fifth story walk up. When I found her apartment, her sister said she had been sick for four days, but no one would come to the area. They were very happy to see me. I made a diagnosis of acute cholecystitis, and I told her what she had to do to get into downstate King's

County Hospital, because she might need an operation. As I was leaving, the lady said that I seemed nice, and that they had not seen a doctor in years. She said her stepson had been killed there for his bag, and she told me that when I went down the stairs not to stop but to just keep going. When she shut the door, I was in the dark. Coming down those stairs I came to the decision that I would stop making house calls. While I had an obligation to my people, I had a moral obligation to seek professional excellence and help people in general, especially those who had the good sense to come and get professional help. I had no business walking around in drug laden areas in the middle of the night and especially walking down five flights of stairs with no lights on, when there was a distinct possibility of getting cracked on the head and being left to die or having my brain scrambled after all those years of sacrifice. As I reached the street, I said to myself, "That's the end of my house call bit."

In my private and personal life, I was having more difficulty with Grace. We were making our lives mutually unbearable. Once she came to the hospital, and I asked her to stay to meet the doctor who had given me the residency who was going to be my chief and teach me my life's work. She left, because she did not like being in a hospital, which was her prerogative. She would not walk through the hospital to meet my friends, because she could not stand the smell of the place. She had always been the sought after and attractive person, and the one who received the most attention, and now, suddenly, as a doctor I was getting more attention and being written about in the papers. She expressed a lot of jealousy. If we went out, she told people what a bad guy I was because I stayed at the hospital, did not take her out, and did not spend enough time with the children. Once we had tickets with friends for a performance at Carnegie Hall and she didn't show. Later she said she was shopping for a long gown. I said that she didn't need a long gown because we were in a box and that anyway few people now wore long gowns to the theater. I said that was it. I told her I was leaving and I would not come back. I stayed away three or four weeks and then she called me and said all was forgiven.

That year I won a prize in Switzerland that paid for a trip back. I thought we could go back and maybe put our marriage back together. When we got to Switzerland, three things happened. First, there were a lot of people who knew me who wanted to take me out to restaurants. After a couple of times, Grace said she did not want to see any of the basketball people anymore, and she wanted me to hang out with some of the nobility that I knew, and the wealthy businessmen and professional people. She thought that was more in keeping with what a doctor should do. I was also taking time off to play basketball with my friends. She said that if I was going to continue to do that, she was going out with a woman from the Belgian nobility she knew. So they went off to visit castles while I went to the café and played basketball.

One day when I was coming back from playing basketball, as I was going up to the United Nations where I used to work in the American Mission, I met this girl. She was driving a little car. I looked up, and it was Nadine. Now Nadine was probably one of the most beautiful women I have ever seen. She had a little peachy face, and she must have been about 5'2." She was sensationally put together, and she was French. Her father was a professor of French. I remembered her from the laboratory. She used to work across the bench from me, right in front of me, and I could not talk to her then because I didn't yet know French for anything but my science classes. She was studying dentistry. I remember once she asked me for a ride over the lunch hour. I didn't know how she had done until that day she stopped me and said, "Wow, it's great to see you." She saw me very little after the first couple of years. We bumped into each other in the hallway, and if she invited me to a party, I would never go. I had basketball and studies and teaching anatomy and the job at the UN, so I did not have time to go to too many parties.

When I saw her on that trip to Switzerland, I told her what I was doing in Geneva and asked if I could see her. She said we could have lunch the next day and talk about what we were doing. We went to one of the little towns on the left bank of Lake Geneva. We ate fish outside and talked for hours about the United States, and I went back through my whole history, including Gretchen, Terry, and Gracie, and all the trouble we were having. She laughed like mad over the Gretchen affair. Anyway, I really loved her company, and so we decided that we would see each other again. I told her that maybe the next night I would call her and make an appointment. I went out with Grace that afternoon, and at night I drove her home and then played some more basketball. She didn't want to come with me and see me play or see the sports guys. So I went out with Nadine, and she took me to a nice place where we danced and talked, and we made love under the stars, and then I came home to Grace. She was upset that I had been out so long, and that was pretty much it. We were finished. The next day we went to see a friend who was having a baby. I had predicted it would come that day and it did. At the bedside, Grace started to get into how ungrateful I was, and that she had put me through school and that I owed her everything. I told her I was the one who had passed the exams and that I had borrowed $10,000 to make sure I was independent. I said I was tired of being the heavy, and I didn't think we would make it. A couple of days later I saw Nadine again. We saw each other a few more times and felt that we really loved each other, but I felt it was too soon to make a commitment, even though I probably loved her the first day I saw her was really glad the years had confirmed her beauty. She was already a practicing dentist then, and she decided she would come to the United States to see what it was like. She needed to see what the black-white situation was like because I would never marry a white girl in Europe and bring her to the United States without her knowing the pressures of the society. I thought that would be unfair. So she said she would come to the United States.

Once we got back to the United States, Gracie continued to find all sorts of things to complain about and new pressures to apply. I thought more and more about Nadine, and I felt for sure that Grace would give me another occasion to leave the house, or she would invite me to leave, because every six or eight months she would come up with a reason and say, "Well, why don't you get out if you don't like it." I just waited until that occasion arose again, and sure enough one summer morning when I was getting ready to go up to Nyack to work in the E.R., she told me she was giving a lawn party for David, who was one of her better friends and also my friend in the past. Dave and his wife and their two children were coming over to my father's yard, and she was going to set it all up. So at 7:30 in the morning, she asked me to call the hospital to get someone to take my place so that I could help set up for the party. I said I was working until four that afternoon and would get to the party about an hour and a half after it started at three. I told her my brothers and sisters would help her set up the party. She said, "No, no, I want you to help me. Get somebody to take your place." So I called about five or six doctors and they all laughed because they already had picnics or dates on that beautiful Sunday. At 8:30 in the morning, I said I was leaving. There was a guy backing me up who had been up all night. She said, "What, do you think the hospital cannot run without you? You are supposed to be such a good doctor. Call up the hospital and tell them that you cannot come because you are sick. Because if you are such a good doctor, they will believe you. You have not ever done that, so do it." At 9:15 I started out of the house and told her I had a commitment to the hospital. So she said, "Well, you never think of the family. It's always the hospital."

At eight that morning some kids had a terrible car accident. There were six of them in the car, and three needed tracheostomies and two needed craniotomies. The hospital had called up people from all over, and the guy who was covering was telling me he was exhausted. I told myself I had to seek professional excellence. When I came home that afternoon, and I saw David there and his wife and the babies and Grace running around and raising hell, I thought that maybe I was responsible for the deaths or three or four people. I saw how Grace and David looked at each other and how happy they were, and I said to myself, "I need to straighten out my life.

This is not going to do." That night Grace repeated that my children missed me and that I didn't spend enough time with them. I told her about the accident. She said, "Well, there was somebody there, wasn't there?" We argued some more, and I explained my ideal of professional excellence, and that I was not going to take what was going on. She then said the famous words that I knew she would say sooner or later: "Well, if you do not like what is going on, then you can just leave. I'll call the children in, and if you don't like what they have to say, then you can leave." So she woke up my children, brought them in and ostracized me in front of them, and I said, "That's it." I did not mean to destroy the kids, and I promised to take care of them from somewhere else.

I left and this time I stayed away, probably because I had been waiting for her to say that to me, a little bit because of the professionalism I was seeking, and a whole lot because of Nadine. I got a letter from Nadine almost on a daily basis with her picture in it, and she told me about what she was doing. I loved the letters she wrote. She described Paris and the streets, and what she was doing in Switzerland, and how she drove in the mountains by herself, and the cars she had, and how she wanted to see me. Then one day I didn't get a letter, and that went on for nine days. I said to myself, "Even if it costs $20, I am going to call Switzerland." I called her house and the operator said to the person on the line that "There is a doctor calling, a man, and he insists on speaking to you." I said that I didn't want to speak to the man, I wanted to speak to Nadine. He said he had to speak to me and that I could not speak to Nadine. I thought about how I told her about how Gretchen's father had played the heavy and now her father was playing the heavy, getting between us. I said that I was going to hang up, but the operator said, the guy seems emphatic and you had better speak to him. I said, "OK," thinking I knew what was going to happen. The operator went off and the man came on and said, "Well, Dr. Johnson, just who are you?" I told him that I went to school with his daughter and I had seen her a few times, and I had written her a few letters, and that I would like to talk to her. "Well," he replied, "Didn't you know that Nadine was in a car accident and she was killed instantly? That is why you cannot talk to her." I told him I very much appreciated him talking to me. I was taken aback and could not say anything else. I could feel his grief. I told him I was hoping she would come to the U.S. It was quite a shock.

Jeanne

I had moved out and was waiting for our divorce to come through. I worked and did a lot of extra work because everyone knew that I was going to be on call and that I did not go home. I moonlighted like moonlighting was going out of style. I moonlighted at Nyack Hospital, Englewood Hospital, Valley Hospital, Montefiore Hospital and back to Brown-Levy Brooklyn and Bronx. I took Allstate insurance calls. I slept four to six hours a night and most of the time I slept two. I did not want to sleep. I did not want to know about sleeping. I wanted only to work, and work was a way of therapy. I liked it when I took care of people. I was living out of the house for about fifteen months. I had a very sick patient, Mrs. Adelman, who was in I.C.U. at Montefiore. She was a beautiful Jewish lady who had ulcerative colitis with toxic mega colon of the large bowel. It perforated before we could get her to surgery. Her intestines were strewn with fecal matter and this led to septicemia that required resection of the large bowel. The operation was successful, though she remained febrile and toxic from the dissemination of gram negative bacteria. Her antibiotics caused a renal shut down that led to circulatory problems and cardiac arrest. She came back from that into a slow sixty-day recovery. Her mind was always beautiful, and she was always thinking about other people in the unit. She had a bed right by the door, and everything that went in and out of the unit she would see. She watched the staff and understood who came late and who came on time, who was harsh and who was gentle, and she soon found out who was married to whom and who was divorced, and who was in love with whom, and all the other things that went on in the unit. It was odd because she was the sick one, yet everyone in the unit came to report their problems to her and she usually had a solution for everyone.

She was a private patient, though I was assigned to care for her. I spent three or four hours every day trying to solve the problems she had. It was in caring for this lady that I got interested in the I.C.U. and in the beautiful nurse who had the most fantastic green eyes set off in in this beautiful angelic face with the kindest smile you could ever wish to see.

Her smile and her laughing eyes were contagious. She raced around the unit, and I loved to see her run from place to place to make sure everyone was comfortable, taking full charge as the lead nurse in a way that was sensitive to everyone's needs and responsibilities. She made things happen. If a patient had a mustache or a beard, she would shave them. Or if a patient was able to eat, she would bring something from her lunch hour for that patient. She was just full of love for life and the human beings she came in contact with. I love people and I love my patients, but it was just heartwarming to see her work with people. She was beautiful through and through. One day I noticed she was eating a tunafish sandwich, and I realized it was Lent and there were a lot of people walking around with ash marks on their foreheads. I asked her why she was eating a tuna sandwich, and she said, "I am eating tuna because I like it." So I said, "Well, that takes care of that." We started to talk to one another, and finally one day I said to her, "What do you do when you leave here? Tonight there is a hospital party. Why don't you come?" She looked at me and said, "I don't know about that." When I was leaving, I asked her one more time why she could not come to the party. She said, "OK, I'll come." So that night I went to the party and stood by the window for maybe three or four hours, but she never showed up at all. The next day I felt unsure if I wanted to talk to her. I thought she might have trouble with the black-white thing, and I looked at her that evening as she was making a call, and I said, "I'll take a raincheck on that party." She said she meant to tell me that a friend of hers had come in from upstate New York, and she had to take her to the city and didn't get back in time to come to the party. I said, "Well, OK, but will you take a raincheck on that party?" She said, "I don't know." I asked her to give me her telephone number so I could call her some time and maybe we could go to a show or something. She said she didn't know. So at the end of the night I was back to see Mrs. Adelman, and Jeanne came up with a little card with her name and telephone number on it. She had mis-spelled her name, and I thought, "Well, that is rough." But I did not give up. She seemed like such a great person. Maybe, I thought, I can finally find someone who can understand what I am trying to do. I thought maybe every moment I spent with her would be worth it, and I looked forward to the next night or lifetime just to be in her presence and to take advantage of that and be happy.

We started to go out. I took her to a nearby Chinese restaurant right after work, and we also went down to Rubin's restaurant in the city to eat. We talked and talked. It was fantastic to talk to her; she listened to what I had to say. Jeanne turned out to be born in Bethlehem, Pennsylvania some fifteen years after me, then moved to Closter, New Jersey, right next to Englewood. She finished high school in South Pasadena, California before her family moved to Pelham Manor, New York. Her dad was a career New York Times newspaper man who had worked in circulation but was now in Chattanooga, Tennessee managing the Chattanooga Times. Her mother was a strong worker for the Presbyterian church. Her paternal grandparents were of Swedish and Irish extraction, and her maternal grandparents Scottish on the one hand and English on the other. Aside from a missionary-type excursion to the Harlem ghetto with her mother's church, Jeanne did not know any black people. She knew there were a few in her school, but she did not know them personally. Despite the black and white difference, and the socio-economic and religious differences, which were enormous, somehow even then I knew Jeanne was forever. Montefiore was her first in life job, and her introduction to the Bronx was to be mugged as she walked home from work one night.

She thought the blacks she worked with were fine. Yes, she enjoyed her work as an R.N. and was saving to buy a blue VW and travel to Hawaii. I asked why not Europe? She answered, "I have no interest in going to Europe or marrying a doctor." I was startled by her reply, but I simply told her I had lived in Europe for eight and a half years playing professional basketball and studying first pharmacy in Italy and then medicine in Geneva. I told her I was fluent in Italian and French. "Why did you go to Europe?" she asked. I said it was a long story, but I had wanted to be a doctor since I was nine, when I was helping my mother clean a doctor's office. I told her how my father couldn't afford to send me to medical school and how he had made it only to sixth grade and mom to third grade. I told her about how my brothers and sisters had worked through college on scholarships and attained three doctoral degrees and three masters' degrees. (Ruth and Sonja earned Ph.D.s. Only in America could that happen. My sister married a white engineer, and my brother Alexander married a white Jewish woman and had bar mitzvahs for his three sons and a bat mitzvah for his daughter. Bob married a white redhead from Montana.) Jeanne said one sister, Meg, had finished Russell Sage College and her other sister, Ellen, was finishing at Franklin Pierce College in New Hampshire. On her father's side, she said they had traced the family back to Swedish nobility; on her mother's side, her grandmother was a member of the Daughters of the American Revolution. I told her I could not trace my heritage back, though I had been told that we had come from a Masai tribe on my father's side and a Bantu tribe on my mother's side. Both sides had mixed with American Indians. I told her my name came from the names of the plantation owners who owned my grandfather. On that first date, I finally noticed the Chinese waiters all walking back and forth. A glance at my watch told me it was a quarter to one, and in that part of the Bronx, that was no place to be at that hour. It was then I decided that I would never take her any place I had not previously checked out. I was already worrying about taking care of her, a job I wanted dearly for the rest of my life.

We were turning in to her street off the Bronx River Parkway, a few minutes from Montefiore Hospital, when she said to me, "I thought you were going to tell me why you went to Europe to study medicine?"

"I thought I was boring you with all that stuff, and the waiters wanted to close. Don't you have a curfew or something? Won't you be tired tomorrow?"

"I missed Johnny Carson, and my shift doesn't start until 3 PM, so unless you have to go, tell me about you and Europe." There we sat in my car in our white uniforms at 1 AM in the morning, talking about European schools and how I got there. I graduated from high school when she was just three years old. I told Jeanne about my neighborhood and my jobs. I told Jeanne about the little jingle we used to sing as kids: if you're white, all right; if you're yellow, you're mellow, if you're brown, stick around; if you're black, get back, get way back. Grammy had been born into slavery, and according to her the only way you could have light skinned children was to be sleeping with the white masters. It was one of Grammy's favorite subjects. No really good Negroes sleeping with white ladies. That just made shit colored people.

I told her about how far too many ministers brought people into the folds with subterfuge, fear and crescendo type preaching where people were threatened with hell, fire and damnation if they did not join the church. You would be asked to stand, and the congregation would start shouting and singing, and then those who belonged to the church were asked to sit down and those remaining standing were asked to come to God, standing alone in the midst of a foggy funk created by body heat and one thousand different perfumes, with tambourines banging, with sisters shouting and fainting like flies, and the rafters swaying and the pews and floors shaking. Only the strong survived, for at this moment the Preacher stomped and danced nine feet tall high up in the pulpit, with his arms flung open stretching to the skies as if he and he alone had the keys to the Pearly Gates, and his voice ranged from a prima-donna high soprano to a bull frog basso as he cajoled, sang and chanted "Bringing in the Sheep." The sheep came; I was one of them. A lot of pastors gave people hope without constructively helping them to move productively and energetically into the mainstream of American life. Not until people like Father Divine from Philadelphia set up schools and provided work did this trend change, and it was pushed along by Martin Luther King and championed by the Reverend Jesse Jackson with his educational PUSH programs. I told her about my neighborhood in Englewood, all the houses and all the people. I talked for hours. Jeanne said, "But you still haven't told me about Switzerland. I have to go now. Anita will be worried about me." I walked her to her apartment, with no thought of kissing on our first date. I was just happy to be with her and her saying as she went in that she wanted to see that street in Englewood.

For weeks after that I waited for her to finish her 3 to 11 shift as Charge Nurse in the medical surgical ICU. Whenever I was with her, she seemed to have time for my every problem, and she listened, no matter what the hour. I could tell her my catastrophes as well as my triumphs. One night she said, "Couldn't you finish your story of how you got to Europe, without my asking?"

"Hey," I responded, "I had to make sure that you wanted to hear the rest." And then I told her about the last place on Armory Street, the Lightning Auto Store, and then about the house where my family lived, all nine of us.

When I listened to her I found we had a lot of things in common, and we really liked each other. Finally I said to her, "Well, I really love you, and I know it is difficult for you to go out with me, and you need to know more about me." So I told her about my two children and my pending divorce. At that point I had another six months to wait before my two years of being out of the house became effective, and the divorce would be in my favor because Grace had sent me out of the house. Jeanne also learned that I was moonlighting on all those nights after I left her. One night I had to go to the Bronx, and I told her that I would pick her up and leave her at home before I went on duty. Well, I picked her up from Montefiore Hospital in the Bronx, and I drove her to downtown Manhattan where she had an apartment, and she refused to get out of the car. She said, "I don't want you working down there, and if you are going to make house calls, I am going with you." I had about four more house calls to make. It was about one o'clock in the morning, but the patients were still waiting because they were very sick, and no doctor would come to their houses. When I came down from one three story building, I looked out the window and saw this beautiful white girl in the middle of a black neighborhood at about three in the morning. She had the lights on and was reading in the car and waiting for me. I remembered coming down from that five-story building where I thought I might get hurt and how I had tried to prove something that doesn't need proving. Then I looked around and saw that it was early Spring and that there were more people on the streets than in the winter, and with those additional people there were certain to be more junkies. And once again I decided to give up house calls as part of my moonlighting.

I began to speculate about how to solve the problem in front of me, and I thought the solution would be not to let so many people come into the city. Maybe people ought to have to prove they had jobs before they could move into the city. If people had stayed in Puerto Rico or the South, they would still be connected to their families, which would keep them in line. Those who came with nothing went on welfare and took no responsibility for their neighbors. Then a lot of them got into drugs.

When I got to the car, I told Jeanne that I was not going to moonlight that way anymore, and she was overjoyed. I really loved her. I told her about my Gretchen affair and my Grace affair and about Nadine, and I told her I would like to live the rest of my life proving how much I loved her and that I would take each day in its turn, trying to love her a little bit more each day. She cried. She was the sensitive person I thought she would be. I did not want to tie her down to the commitment of marriage if we were not going to get married. I didn't see any reason for upsetting her parents or anyone else in her family. If we were just going to see each other, then why bring that grief to them without having them understand that we had decided that we were going to love each other and that we wanted to see each other for the rest of our lives. So I refused to go out and meet her parents.

My feelings for her came from an ordinary and mundane attraction for her obvious physical beauty, but it was her unpretentious, natural way of coming across as a person of deep inner goodness and beauty that filled me completely. I knew that the time had come for me to live my life for one person. For whatever reason, God had determined that she would be white. I loved her and it hurt, and I wondered at His wisdom as I had no right to do and had never done before. I also thought it was the proximity of our working together that connected us, as well as the artificially elevated and often unwarranted and privileged position of the doctor in the hospital hierarchy.

The hospital world permits and seemingly expects the doctor to comport himself as a spoiled brat. All too often the nurses, generally female, hold open the doors for the doctors, generally male. Frequently the nurses run at the snap of a doctor's fingers, like scurrying pack animals, toting equipment and material behind the doctor, or bringing it over to the bedside while the doctor waits or carries nothing. The O.R. is a total dictatorship. Life and death drama takes place in the O.R. as in no other place in the hospital, and that the doctor must be in charge is no overstatement. Yet inexcusable are the childish eruptions of screaming, name-calling, rank sarcasm and throwing of instruments. Many times doctors ignore the good ideas, observations, and judgments that emanate from a nurse, just because she is a nurse. Because of that caste system, I was determined to know Jeanne outside the medical world.

We had tickets to a downtown show one night. I had been going out with two or three other girls strictly for fun, but no matter whom I went out with or whatever I did, I always thought about Jeanne as someone special. I found myself falling more and more in love with her, and I thought that perhaps we should do some other things to see how she would react to being out with a black person. I had been very selective about where I would take her. We had been going to Rubin's, which was a great restaurant in the city famous for its juicy steaks, and we went to little Chinese and Italian places in the Bronx. We would sit down for hours and talk about almost anything. We talked a lot about work. I did not have to forget about work. We talked about the things we were doing in the I.C.U. and what I was doing in surgery. She loved medicine. One day I felt we had to do something else like go to the theater and a basketball game to expose her to the general public and see how our relationship stood up underneath social onslaughts. So I got two tickets to "Promises, Promises," but on the day of the performance I had to give a speech at a university on goals other than professionalism for athletes. I asked Jeanne to give the tickets to someone who might want to go, or to her mother and father if she could not think of anyone else. Her parents went and thought it was a fantastic show, and who was I that could get such fantastic tickets. She told them I was a black doctor at the hospital she had been dating. There was a silence in the home for a moment, and then her mother said she should invite me to dinner to meet me. Her father agreed.

They asked me to dinner, but I always found an excuse not to come. I thought, why should I create this problem for Jeanne unless we are really going to get married. If we were only going to date, then I saw no need to disturb her mother and father with fears of black and white relationships. So I never went to their house. Her father then accepted a job in the South with the Chattanooga Times, and he was gone a good bit of the time. Her mother went down to stay with him for a while, and in the interim, Jeanne had to run the house. She had two younger sisters, Ellen and Meg. Jeanne worked her eight or ten-hour shift at the hospital and then went home to sleep, cut the grass, wash the windows, cut the hedges and everything else. She had boundless energy. She tried to get me to come over, but I always told her that I had not met her mother and father, so I would not come to her house. Finally, she said that I was going to have to come to the house or I was not going to see her, because she had to take care of her sisters. I was a bit of a chicken to go. I got four sets of tickets and took my friend Ron and his girlfriend Carol, who were both white, and we all went to pick up Jeanne. I went to the door and rang, and Meg came to the door and said, "Come in. I've heard all about you." I was not sure of that was good or bad. I went into the living room. It was a nice, comfortable home in Pelham Manor on one of the larger lots. I went into the kitchen, and Meg's little sister Ellen was there with about three or four girlfriends, and everybody looked up at me. Some looked surprised. Some looked startled, and others just smiled. I picked up Ellen and said, "Hi," and then left with Jeanne.

We went down and saw "Promises, Promises," and then we went out and sat and talked. Ron was another chief resident in general surgery, like me, and there was lots to talk about. Both the girls were nurses, and we were oblivious as to any remarks or looks that might have been passed around us. Jeanne was such a blithe spirit. As time went on, we found a little French restaurant where we could dance and went there often with other couples. We walked in Central Park and went to theater and ballets and basketball games and for long rides. We watched the leaves changing colors, and we had incessant conversations about black and white in this country, and about marriage and about the things we needed and wanted in life. I felt bad when I was not in her company. We consolidated our love by searching for all the pitfalls that usually bog down a black and white relationship. In essence we felt that we loved each other, and that was the important thing. We were sorry for the inconvenience or the sadness that we were causing other people and the problems we were creating in our racist society. Those were problems outside our relationship, and that was where we were going to keep them. We felt that we wanted to get married.

We were waiting for my divorce to come through. One day Jeanne was driving my car. Her Volkswagen had been stolen, so we rented a car. That car got a flat tire, so I loaned her mine. Jeanne was driving down the West Side Highway when Grace saw her. Grace followed her until Jeanne stopped at a gas station on 96th Street. Grace hopped out and went over to the window of my car and said, "What are you doing in my husband's car?" Jeanne said, "My car was stolen, so I borrowed his car." Jeanne took Grace to her house and they talked about me. Up until that point, Gracie was willing to file the divorce in my favor. Grace felt I was not happy and had asked me to leave the house, but she figured I did not have anyone else and was probably going to stay unhappy and be married to medicine and surgery. When she found out that I had found someone and that we loved each other, Grace came back and made more demands. She also went to my friends and told them what a creep I was, and she tried to tie up the divorce. Her lawyers stuck me up for another eight thousand dollars, for a total of $40,000 plus a couple thousand more in lawyers' fees and a promise to cover the education of my children through university. I wasn't sure how I was going to be able to pay for all this additional financial burden.

Jeanne and I talked about it, and we decided that after she had met and talked with Grace we really did love one another. We didn't argue about the money that had to be paid out. It was money that I certainly was not making at the time. Only God and love would allow me to make it in the future. Jeanne's thought was that we were not paying Grace, we were paying to be free so that we could have one another. Once all that was established, the divorce was set to go through in early May, and we had to tell Jeanne's parents that we were going to get married. I still had not gone over to meet them in spite of their persistent invitations to dinner. Jeanne got sick, and I would not let anyone else take care of her. Jeanne was still taking care of her parents' house while her mother was down in Chattanooga with her father. I went to see Jeanne and took lab samples and gave her medication for a high fever and abdominal pain. Meanwhile, her little sister panicked and called their mother in Chattanooga, and her mother flew back. Jeanne would not see anyone but me, so her mother called me. I came to the house and went to the back door, where Meg let me in. I walked into the living room, and Mrs. Holmberg had three or four families over, and they were chatting. So I walk in black, and everyone else is white, and Mrs. Holmberg says, "Oh, you are Dr. Johnson," and she introduced me to everyone else. She said, "This is my daughter's doctor." I said "hi" to everyone and asked Mrs. Holmberg if she wanted to come upstairs to examine Jeanne, and she said no. When I saw Jeanne, I said, "What's happening? You're going to get me in trouble over here. Your mother has got the whole neighborhood in the house downstairs." She laughed and asked me what her mother said to me. I told her that her mother was very nice. I examined her, and her temperature was down and her chest was clear. Then I said we could not spend too much time upstairs, so I kissed her and left.

I went downstairs. The guests had gone and her mother was waiting for me. We sat and talked, and she was a super individual who thought it was nice that I would find time to come over and take care of Jeanne. She thanked me for the tickets to the show, and she asked why I had not come to dinner. I told her there was a lot going on, and perhaps another time. She responded that she was going to call her husband and make arrangements right then. She called Tennessee, and I spoke to Jeanne's father, who thanked me for caring for Jeanne. He sounded like a great guy. I came back each morning before I went on duty and took blood and urine and talked to her mother for about three or four days. After Jeanne was well, she and her mother went to Chattanooga for a long rest of about fifteen days. For me, each day was worse than then last. Finally, she returned. I asked her what her mother had said, and Jeanne replied that her mother was upset because I came in the back door. She knew that blacks hated coming in back doors, so why had I? That was the only remark her mother had made about our relationship.

At that time, I was working a rotation in the middle of the Spanish Black ghetto in the South Bronx. I was talking to an x-ray tech about some films, and out of the elevator pop three people: Jeanne and her mother and father. Her mother was wearing a mink stole and her father had on a very fine cashmere coat. They stood there looking at me in this sea of blacks and Puerto Ricans. I said, "Gosh, what brought you here?" Jeanne said, "Well my father has a shoulder pain, and he wants you to read the x-rays and say what needs to be done." Her mother said, "I think he has bursitis." Sure enough, I read the x-rays and there were little flecks of calcium around the rotary cuff, and her mother had made a perfect diagnosis. I put her father on some exercise and some pain medications. I walked him out of the hospital that day and around the corner. They were not worried about what might happen to them in that neighborhood in the evening. Mr. Holmberg turned out to be a great guy, about 6'3," a strapping Swedish man. I said to myself, "Wow, Jeanne really comes from some great stuff. Her mother and father are beautiful people." They invited me to dinner again, and this time I accepted. It was Thanksgiving Dinner. Each of the girls was allowed to invite a friend. Their mother asked them what they thought of their sister dating a black man and if there would be any trouble with their dates. The middle daughter said, "If my date cannot understand and accept my sister going out with a black doctor, then he is not worth dating." The little one said, "Nowadays we are mod, and it does not really matter if you are black or white. It's not important. We are used to seeing things like that."

I thought it was extraordinary that their mother asked, that she was thinking about all of her daughters and their welfare. I appreciated that she could be sensitive to my needs and my socio-economic position. I started to go often to the Holmberg household to see Jeanne, take her out, or stay and watch television. I spent a lot of evenings at her home. Finally, Jeanne and I decided that when the divorce came through we would get married. I went to her father and sat down and told him that I was 37 years old and Jeanne was 23, and I would like to have his blessing for our marriage. Before I could say anything, he said, "I know what you have to talk about, and I want you to know that Dot and I are 100% behind you. We love our daughter, and we respect her ability to decide who is a good person and who is not a good person, and if she loves you, that is enough for us. We just want her to be happy and you to be happy." I told him that I was in the process of getting a divorce that was supposed to go through in May. It was then about April,

Eastertime. I met with my lawyer almost every day to get the divorce pushed through. I told Jeanne's father that he could see that I was black, and that there was a fifteen-year age difference. I was going into practice, and I was not sure what kind of money I would make, but I could take care of her. He replied that the situation was a little rougher than he thought it would be, but what he said still went, and he and her mother would stand behind us. He said that the only problem in the family might be the grandparents, who had not known any blacks and who tended to do what most people in the country did: pigeonhole people. I said I understood how people in that age group could have negative feelings about blacks. I couldn't tell them what to think because I didn't know what personal experiences they had. I would not be unhappy if they did not change their minds about black people or even didn't want to have anything to do with me. I wanted Jeanne to be happy, and if she could do that, it would be all right, though I would rather that she have a working relationship with her grandparents. Mr. Holmberg said he would arrange a meeting so that we could talk about it, and that his Presbyterian minister would like to talk to me about the issues that Jeanne and I might face, though he understood that we had probably talked about all of the issues. Still, if there was something we had overlooked, we could face those issues with the minister. Mr. Holmberg was just beautiful, straightforward and honest. He was the way that people should be, but 99% of people are not. He was great, not because he agreed to let me marry his daughter, but because he, in our racist day and age, could see that the most important thing was to find someone to love and live with.

Jeanne and I went to see the minister. He turned out to be another wonderful guy who was not pushing us in one direction or another. We went over the things that Jeanne and I had discussed: the black and white thing and how we were attracted to each other. Was it because we were not supposed to be attracted, or because we worked together in the hospital, or that we were attracted because of sexual fantasies, and all the other things we had talked about in restaurants and on walks on the streets and sitting in the woods. We had really gone over these things with each other and we realized that it would be no easy task, but that we would work on it every day, and by working on it lead people together alongside us and behind us. Some people from West Virginia and Georgia and Chattanooga came to talk to us, not to ask questions, but to question us instead with their eyes and go away seeming satisfied that we were the exception to the rule or to their rule anyway. People who came in contact with us or talked to us were always friendly, no matter how we may have come in contact. The end result was that people were happy for having stopped and talked to us. Our happiness was contagious and affected anyone who came around us. Jeanne and her parents chose a weekend to go up to Connecticut to meet both sets of grandparents without me. Jeanne had told them that she had fallen in love with a black man and that he was a doctor, and she told them about the things I had done. She also said that she was sorry, but she loved me and that we were going to get married. Her speech was greeted with silence. Mrs. Holmberg went to the phone and called me. I was waiting in my room at the Montefiore to hear from them. She said the grandparents had heard about me, and would I please come up to dinner in two weeks.

In two weeks, I went up and met Jeanne's uncle Mack and his wife Janice and their children, and relatives from all over the country. They had a party, and each one came over and talked to me for ten or fifteen minutes about what I had been doing and where I was going and what it was all about. They talked to me sincerely as hard-working people, and they appreciated the fact that I worked hard to try to make something of myself, and we were instant friends. The bond that tied us was the bond of hard work. Each one of the family had done something with their lives and worked hard to achieve what they had accomplished. We got along great. I went home surprised that I had found an entire family in the United States that was at least in control of their prejudices.

I wanted us to get married in Geneva, because Geneva had meant so much to me. I had earned my doctorate there, and played basketball, and I knew lots of people. When we left for Europe, my divorce had not yet come through. I had only one month of vacation, and Jeanne had also worked so that she had one month of vacation. We were not sure when we could go again. We already had our plane tickets, though the court was still holding up the divorce. Mrs. Holmberg said she felt we should go. We were adults and we loved each other. We were going to get married, and the divorce would come through. Her father also wanted us to go, though at the airport he said quietly to me, "I want you to take care of my daughter." He could not have charged me with a more precious obligation.

The week prior to leaving, I had taken Jeanne over to my mother's house. She was furious that I was getting a divorce, because she had thought all along that Grace and I would get back together, even after the separation. There had been no divorces in our family. She had raised six children, and she did not understand. She was extremely upset at the prospect of my marriage to Jeanne, and she treated Jeanne very shabbily. I told her that if she was going to treat Jeanne that way, she would not see me again until she had made up her mind that this was the woman I loved. I told her that though Grace was a good woman, and we were married, and I knew what that meant to her religiously, we were not making each other happy. We were disrupting the lives of our children, and they were suffering because of the bad atmosphere in the house. It took a while until my mother could talk to Jeanne at all. Just before we went to Geneva, I went over and told my mother and father that Jeanne and I were getting married. Jeanne's parents saw us off at the plane. We landed in Paris not knowing whether I was divorced or not divorced, and we went to a small town outside Paris. It was great to show Jeanne all the things I thought were beautiful in Europe. I spoke fluent French and Italian, so it was easy to order in restaurants and talk to people in the streets.

Next day we drove to Brussels, where I called my friend Jerry back in the States who had gone to school with my brother. He told me that my divorce had come through on June 2, as predicted. I thanked him, and I cried. We called Geneva and made arrangements to be married. There was a huge amount of red tape. Nevertheless, a friend I used to play basketball with married us. The ceremony was simple. The witnesses were a few of my friends, all of us gathered around a big table. During the ceremony Jeanne began to cry and hold on to my hand tighter. She was the only one who couldn't understand French, and the minister could sense that she felt in that moment lost and left out of the ceremony because of the language and because she was some 6,000 miles from her relatives, and only my friends were there. He switched to English, though his English was not that good. It was beautiful that he could size up the situation and go right into English and finish the ceremony perfectly. We went out that night, and we spent the rest of the month driving around. We got up early and had breakfast at sunrise. Some nights we ate in plush restaurants; other days we ate in the fields. We had no schedule and no hotel reservations. Some nights we slept in the best places; some nights we slept with friends. We drove some 5,000 miles in thirty days, all along the Alps from Germany, through East and West Germany and Czechoslovakia and Austria and then into Italy and back to Geneva. We never tired of one another. We enjoyed talking with the people we met along the way in cafes and restaurants. They came into our lives for brief moments and imparted good wishes.

Settling In

When we got back to the United States, I decided that I would not see Chino and Renee because I did not want them polarized into two camps or jumping between two camps, and because I felt that Grace would take care of them. She was a good woman, and she would be able to raise them to be good kids without any confusion. I had my surgical residency to complete, which did not allow much time for anything, as I was on every other night and moonlighting. It was impossible for me to participate in bringing up two teenagers. I couldn't do both. I had gone this far into surgery, I had left the house long ago, I was married to Jeanne, and I simply had no more time. Jeanne was beautiful. She came to be with me while I was working. She was sensitive enough to become part of the work I was doing. She knew that what made me function was my driving desire to obtain professional excellence. I was addicted to work, and she made herself part of my work.

My children knew that my door was open. They could always come and visit me, and as they got older they would come to understand that two very good people may not be suited for marriage, which was the case with me and Grace. The way I handled any hostility was to send cards and to make sure they had enough money. I remembered them at birthdays and Christmas and let them know where they could reach me. It was a hard choice, but I thought I was making the best of a bad situation. Jeanne and I wondered about having children: a white lady having a black child come from her. We talked about it, and Jeanne was not ready for it. She felt that she did not know how to raise a black child; that was her first approach to it. Finally, after we had been married for over a year, she said to me one day, "I am ready to have your child, and I know we will make it. We love each other, and we will be able to instill that love in our child so that he will be able to live and have a chance for happiness in this country." She stopped taking birth control pills, and she wanted to have a baby. I felt that was great. I had another year and a half of residency, so I thought we could do the rhythm system and make sure we didn't have any children until I was finished. She never had another period after that conversation. We felt that Jaime was thought about, contrived and conceived in love, and for that reason we call him Jamie, which is really J'aime, or "I love" in French. It was typical of Jeanne that she wanted to have this baby by natural childbirth. My fear was that we might have a girl child and that I would not know how to relate to a girl and to help her, especially in American black society. I prayed that we would have a boy, and God sent us that boy.

I thought back to the day Jaime was born. What a glorious day! All the Irish nurses in that Jewish hospital were betting that this half-black baby would be born on St. Patrick's Day, and he was. We were all elated. I was the Montefiore's first American born black chief resident of general surgery, and now I was one of four hundred applicants chosen for the two cardiac surgical residency positions, making me the first black to do cardiac surgery at Montefiore. I was proud.

On the day Jaime was born, I was helping Dr. Attai replace an aortic valve. No matter how tired I was, or how much sleep I did not get, I never failed to have all my senses jolted awake by the responsibility of surgery. That great awakening started as I flung open the O.R. door. Once inside the operating suite, it was teamwork, unrestrained goal-oriented, purposeful movement. There was no wasted movement. The O.R. was a world unto itself of unending excitement. Clean, starched, green uniforms were piled to the ceiling. Mr. Brown, a pleasant, round black man was responsible for seeing that all the uniforms, boots, masks and hoods were in place. He did his job with dignity and genuine concern for all the doctors. He was proud of his menial but important job. Job segregation was definite. Doctors, nurses and professionals were white, and ancillary help was almost 100% black. I was a mutation.

Even dressing and undressing in the O.R. was exciting in its atmosphere. There was a sense of urgency and an abhorrence for waste of time. This feeling snowballed as I moved out of the dressing room into the scrub room, where I was greeted by the pump techs and orderlies, who were generally black. I always wore a distinctive headband that Jeanne had made for me, kiddingly saying that it would eliminate the need for any nurse to mop my brow. There was also a lot of kidding because the O.R. crew had adopted me as their doctor, and for them I was a symbol of black progress. After six years I had earned their respect. The first time I had walked into the surgical ward, the head nurse and some private duty nurses asked me what patient I was specialling that night, explaining to me the pecking order as

I played along that I was a private duty nurse, until I had to answer a page for Dr. Johnson. I remember them gasping, but it was a cause for much laughter and a wonderful bond between us in the years that followed. It was years before some of the older blacks and whites could say anything but "Mr. Johnson." When they finally said, "Dr. Johnson," I just lightly said, "You got it." To myself, whatever I was called, I knew who I was, I knew what I was doing, where I was going, and that I had one permanent partner, and that was God Himself.

While scrubbing, I'd pray to God to let me be an instrument of good and to guide my fingers. "If I can't help, don't let me hurt." Then I'd make a mental check of the individual patient's laboratory results, cath data, clinical findings, and specific complaints. I'd go over probable anatomy, the problems that might arise from the pathology that would be there, what steps I might take to avoid trouble, and what I could do immediately to get out of trouble. A fast mental check of all necessary instruments invariably followed. Next would be a discussion of our surgical plan A through Z with the other resident, and we'd briefly wonder whether the attending would let me do the entire case. I did fifty-seven such cases in my last year as Resident in Cardiac Surgery. All the while, our eyes were glued to the other side of the glass window through which we were constantly observing the patient. Completing the scrub, we would enter the O.R.

After speaking to the anesthesiologist and the resident who would help me start the case, I would reassure the patient, give the signal for the patient to be put to sleep, put the C.V.P. in the heart, and put in the arterial line, a line in the arm, and a Foley catheter for urinary output. Then I would scrub the patient clean, paint him and drape him sterile, so the scenario for surgery was set.

Our gloves were pulled in place. I positioned the lights over the patient, asked for the scalpel, and with one smooth, decisive motion made an incision from the base of the neck to the umbilicus. The first swift incision never failed to excite me. We controlled the bleeding by electrical coagulation. I took a vertical saw and with a ripping and buzzing sound cut through the bony sternum. We worked furiously to control bleeding, and this busy work introduced us into a suspended hypnotic state, where our minds were programmed to shut out all else, and I mean all personal problems, real, unreal, imagined, or even eventual. It was the moment of truth that we, the surgical team, gave ourselves totally to finding the health-giving solution to this one patient's problem at this moment in time and space. Once bleeding was controlled, the split sternum was pried open, like a coconut. There before us, our intense concentration was momentarily jarred by the everlasting beauty of the naked beating heart. We sutured purse strings at two areas on the beating right atrium. It is a singular art to sew on the beating heart without spilling blood. We did it two or three times a day. We made an opening in the middle of these circles, slipped in plastic tubes, and tied them firmly in the heart. Once the plastic tubes were in, they were connected to the heart-lung machine. Another weighty moment was experienced when the heart-lung machine was turned on, the heart was instantaneously sucked empty of all its blood, and I knew the patient's life was suspended in time. It was God, the pump, and the cardiac team all working to give this patient a better life.

Dr. Attai evaluated the diseased aortic valve. It was resected out, and an artificial one was chosen and sutured into place. I was engrossed in the mechanics of reconstructing the aorta and listening for any discord in the rhythms put forward by the continuous electrocardiographic, electroencephalographic, respiratory and heart-lung machine monitors. Startled by a sharp tap on the shoulder, I was annoyed to find Jerry, an O.R. scrub technician, standing behind me. Jerry was definitely not one of my favorite people. He was a twenty-ish year old black male who was an extroverted, self-announced, devoted homosexual. He was the boisterous leader of a mushrooming band of black queens. Whenever he scrubbed, he would pull on my gloves really slowly; then, instead of the sharp, crisp and traditional surgical passing of instruments, he would place them slowly, lingeringly and gently into my hand. Adding insult to injury, his numerous bedfellows would flit in and out, chirping about their adventures. Before the delicate pump time started, I usually said in a flat, expressionless monotone, "Ladies, in or out, and no noise please." They were the thorny part of the rose that was the group of hard-working O.R. staff. I simply glared as I thought, how dare this ass hole touch me. Finally, as he repeated himself with his high-pitched effeminate voice, I understood what he was saying, which was, "You wife called to say she had a bloody show, and that if you don't hurry, she will have the baby at home." Dr. Attai freed me and the second assistant became the first assistant as I bolted from the O.R.

Still buttoning my white resident's shirt, I ran through the long halls and finally plunged into the low, narrow tunnel that was the umbilical cord that led from the bowels of the hospital to the basement of our apartment house. While the tunnel connected the hospital with my apartment, for six years it had often disconnected me from the entire world. Once I was on duty for eleven straight days, during which I arrived in darkness, left in darkness, and never knew if it was raining, snowing or cold, and for long periods did not know if it was day or night, because there were no windows in the O.R. or the Recovery Room. I would have a day off, and suddenly it was Spring!

I cursed the tunnel because it was so low that I had to bend my 6'5" frame and could not run. I had bumped my head any number of times racing to get to a cardiac arrest. The Montefiore Hospital was located in the North Bronx, which was once a solidly white community and a mostly Jewish district that was being taken over by Puerto Ricans and blacks. The Hospital is a Jewish Federation hospital. I knew I was accepted there when some of the old timers started to tell me about the anti-Semitism practiced by some of the great old waspy-Anglo hospitals in the City and how the Jewish Federation had set up their own hospitals to ensure training of their own people, and didn't I agree that there were too many foreigners being trained at Montefiore and thereby depriving good Jewish boys of Class A training? I had come to Montefiore by accident. The medical school at Geneva had given me a recommendation to Harvard, where I was told I could do my internship if I were willing to complete my last year of medical school there and then stay for two years of internship instead of one. I couldn't afford that. I decided that after living in clean, green Geneva, I couldn't deal with Columbia, either.

On the day Jaime was born, I had been at Montefiore for six years. I thanked God that the elevator was empty and waiting. Getting off on the fifth floor, I pushed open the door into our studio. I was all wonderment as one look at Jeanne's clear eyes staring out at me from her beautiful mask of pregnancy wiped out all my anguish and anxiety. How amply pregnant she was. No matter what the circumstances, she was always right for them. I imagined her at a debutante ball with two or three hundred girls, all dressed in long gowns and she in her dungarees making them feel overdressed. She quickly read the feelings on my face and said, "I didn't want to go to the hospital too soon. As a nurse, I'd feel like a fool being sent home for false labor. I'm between contractions." She continued, "Do you want to examine me?" "No way," I blurted, "Please let's get to the hospital."

"First, we are stopping by Dr. Winston's, who will make sure it's time for me to go. He's waiting for us." On the way over in the car, we went through the La Maze skills we had acquired in the previous six weeks of unforgettable classes. The childbirth without pain system had brought us even closer, which in itself seemed almost impossible. Meeting once a week with six other couples who were facing the same hopes and fears of childbirth was a singularly fulfilling experience that made us all kinsmen of a sort. The true joy and value, though, was the breathing and physical exercises we did together at home while gleaning some time for ourselves totally away from the urgencies of the hospital and devoting our thoughts to this person coming into the lives of the two of us. Dr. Winston examined Jeanne, shook his head smiling, and said, "Do you have to see the whites of the baby's eyes before you know it's coming? Get to the hospital, lady."

As we wove in and out of traffic making our way to the Albert Einstein hospital, I was glad that I had chosen and that Jeanne approved of Dr. Winston as her obstetrician. Our first meeting had been a middle of the night event. I had called him to get me out of a jam several years before, and we had scrubbed together. I knew he was a good surgeon. Montefiore had only gynecology but no obstetrical service. One night when I was off duty and home in bed, one of the female interns had called me to come and examine her, as she would let only me do the exam. I was hard put to explain this to Jeanne, but I am sure it was because that doctor and I had worked together in Morisania, and she had seen me operate many times. We had often taken moonlighting together and had talked about her home country, which was Czechoslovakia, where I had played many times. Examining her, I found she had a tubal pregnancy. I called a prominent gynecologist from the Montefiore staff. He came unwillingly to the E.R. where he declared that the drop in the woman doctor's hematocrit was due to her menstrual period, and her pain was due to pelvic inflammatory disease. He refused to consider tubal pregnancy. I called our surgical director and told him what I thought, and he recommended Dr. Winston from Albert Einstein and gave him emergency privileges. Winston operated and found a bleeding tubal pregnancy. He did a superb job. So when Jeanne became pregnant, I naturally thought of him.

In the labor room, it was about five o'clock in the evening. Whew, whew, whew she went with each contraction, and I went whew, whew, whew with her and changed the cadence to distract her from the discomfort she was experiencing between contractions. This went on for hours, and I wondered at her strength. Between contractions, I held her hand. I looked out at the New York skyline where the sun was setting in the West, causing a beautiful dark pink waist band with a reddish orange sun like a buckle placed around the buildings, which seemed, with the sun behind them to be so many oddly shaped oblong black boxes without windows looking at the horizon. There were a thousand hues of purples, blues and pinks, while rising in the East was a pumpkin colored full moon gigantic when compared to the to the manmade objects on the Earth. The buildings on the east side had just begun to turn on a million and one lights of varied brilliance and a miracle of different yellows. They looked like stars in an asphalt sky. Jeanne went whew, whew, whew, and I joined her, marveling at how well she controlled herself. A beautiful child giving birth to a beautiful child.

Strange how in New York City this beautiful time of dusk heralds the darkness of night when the animals take over. Shark-like they strike down the unsuspecting and the unaware. Awareness and purposeful movement at the keys to surviving and enjoying a New York City night. The return of daylight bustles in the normal people who energetically reclaim the city for another day.

My hand, which rested gently on Jeanne's abdomen, sensed strong rhythmic breathing and a sustained contraction. As the contraction subsided and Jeanne gathered her strength, my thoughts turned to how we first met.

One night nine months before when we had made love and I was suspended between heaven and earth, I heard her whisper, "I have stopped taking the pill because I am ready to have your baby. I love you and I want your baby." I hugged her and said, "Now that sure was a statement," and we laughed. Jeanne had another contraction, and her ability to use each one effectively hastened the birth of Jaime. As I dressed in a green, sterile suit to join her in the delivery room, I prayed for a normal child, remembering full well the time in Geneva when I had assisted at the birth of a hydrocephalic monster. That child had to be delivered by Caesarean section because of the size of its head, and as I left the O.R., I ran into one of the basketball players from the university team who asked if I had assisted in the Caesarean section birth of his child. He wanted to know if it was a boy or a girl. Remembering only the protruding forehead on a head that seemed so big that for all intents and purposes it was ready to burst at any moment, remembering the tiny, tiny eyes that were like blue suns half way up on the horizon in a huge white sky, I heard him repeat the question: Is it a boy or a girl? Shuddering again, I found myself saying that I would go with him to see the baby, because I knew he would need help. Seeing the baby, he burst into tears and then sat quietly for several minutes. Then in a crescendo his voice pled with me to kill the child and sobbingly asked me not to show the child to his wife. The child died in several weeks. It was fed only water; we did nothing else to keep it alive.

With such memories tormenting me, I went trembling to the O.R., determined not to let my fears filter through to Jeanne. Helping Jeanne with her pushing and assisting in every way I could, I uttered my heartfelt prayers for a healthy child. Finally, the head crowned, the stark white vulva tensed by the unrelenting push of the curly black hair of the infant. Suddenly Dr. Winston was speckled with blood as he had deftly done a lateral episiotomy. Jeanne was consumed by the vision of the birth of our child and felt no pain as blood squirted everywhere and the head popped through, followed by the flip of the first shoulder and then the other. The baby cried while still in the vagina and not yet completely born. The shoulder was so large and squared, the arms and hands so long and huge that I thought that if this is a girl, she would certainly be around the house forever. The baby rotated and the genitals popped out, and to our everlasting joy it was a boy, a boy born totally white with only his scrotum being the blackest of blacks to match his black curly hair. We cried.

We got back to the post-delivery room exhausted by the joyful event of birth. Happy and feeling eternally blessed for having a normal child. Jeanne said, "I only have girl names. I thought you said you wanted a girl?"

"Je t'aime," I said to her in French. "I love you," I repeated in English. "I knew you'd give me a boy, but I knew we'd manage if we had a girl. I was just making sure you would not be upset. Let's name him Bill after your father."

"No," she said, "He looks like a Fletcher III with those big feet and large hands."

"OK," I said, "But we'll call him Jaime, which to us will take the French meaning of I love (J'aime) because he was born out of love."

It was less than ten minutes after childbirth and Jeanne had already walked the thirty odd yards to the nursery window, and now we were holding on to each other walking back in the beautiful silence that often engulfed us in which I felt her every vibration. I felt her spiritually crawl up inside of me; I felt her gently shake my tree of life; I felt her curl up inside my heart causing it to feel pleasantly heavy and to ache with joy.

I had kissed her and left the hospital still wrapped up in the allure of birth until the blasting horns of the traffic made me realize I was now off course for the Montefiore Hospital. I made a U-turn to get back to the grand concourse. I was disturbed by the thought that our helpless, innocent child, without sins, without trespasses, would be hated, suppressed, prejudiced against and denied so many things in our society because of his being born into the most highly identifiable minority. It suddenly came to me that the greatest man I had ever known was my father. I made another U-turn. This time I headed for Englewood where I had grown up. I noticed my speed increasing as I crossed the George Washington Bridge like some stable horse who smells some oats in the barn and turns the bend some quarter of a mile away. As I drove down the hilly palisades I remembered that the luxurious mansions housed people who called the black ghetto "Little Texas," and the greening period of my life came back as if I had never left.

Jaime's uninhibited, infectious, infant pure laughter was a happy sound even at two in the morning. Although it was Jaime's first birthday, I had to do my moonlighting job at the Raritan Valley Hospital. On call for 24 straight hours, I was both the house doctor and the emergency room doctor in this 125-bed hospital. After being on duty at the Montefiore Hospital every day and every other night and every other weekend, this was an especially grueling assignment, but Jaime's bubbling, cascading laughter was both relaxing and therapeutic.

The nurses in the E.R. had given him a St. Patrick's day and birthday party all rolled into one. He had reciprocated by taking his first solo steps. Jeanne had fallen asleep. I kissed her gently. She turned, her beautiful green eyes opened, and she smiled that "all's right with the world" smile. She was beautiful not because her eyes were beautiful, her hair was beautiful, but because when she smiled, her face shone with her inner beauty. I wondered how she had the energy to follow me around while I worked as E.R. physician in the Englewood, Morrisania, Nyack, Raritan Valley hospitals and made house calls in Brooklyn and insurance physicals in the Bronx in addition to my regular residency. I allowed myself five nights a month of freedom and sleep. Jeanne had come along everywhere when she was not on duty as ICU-Clinical supervisor. She worked at Montefiore until Jaime was born. Now she came on weekends and brought Jaime. Jeanne fell quickly to sleep again, but Jaime was ready to play.

I tossed him in the air again and again. He loved it. Seeing him so happy and innocent, I held him close to me, wishing I could protect him forever. How would he function in our one-upmanship society where he was part of the highly identifiable minority? I remembered the St. Patrick's Day of the year before when Jaime was born and the tape I had dictated on that day as a letter to give him for his twenty-first birthday. In that moment of peace and truth, I suddenly realized that the most important gift my father had given to me I must at all costs pass on to my son. This was the gift of learning to love one's own self, to have self-respect, and to have quiet, strong, unwavering dignity and self-determination. My dad simply said, "If you can love yourself, that is what God expects and is a quota. Anyone else loving you is a surplus. Don't worry about people hating, liking or loving you. Just do the right things and God will love you and guide you."

Ambush and Aftermath

There is a malignancy eating at the very heart and soul of most of the hospitals in the northeastern United States. That cancer is gatekeeping, locking out or keeping out physicians from hospital staffs and getting rid of as many competitors as possible. This abomination of over-zealous and often illegal gatekeeping is spurred by the creation of new US medical schools and the enlargement of medical schools already in existence. This combination of forces spews out well trained and talented physicians who challenge the power groups already established within hospitals, who seek to control monopolies by means of gatekeeping.

On February 10, 1987, my privileges to perform thoracic and vascular surgery at Nyack Hospital were summarily suspended without any hearing, warning, or any notice of charges against me. I was not even told that meetings to suspend my privileges would be held. The suspension was based on a "review" of my cases by my only competitor in cardio-thoracic surgery. That "review" did not identify any deficiency for any patient, nor did it say what criteria were being employed. My competitor later admitted that he and he alone decided what to call an error and that he also reviewed his own cases. I found and documented collusion, conspiracy, fraud, suppressive malice, denial of constitutional rights, denial of human rights, denial of rights under hospital by-laws and regulations, and denial of my right of due process.

After nineteen years of working at Nyack Hospital and fourteen years in private practice I was asked to resign my privileges in vascular and thoracic surgery. In that fourteen years, I performed three hundred surgical cases per year, which adds up to some 4200 cases. I did not have one malpractice case settled against me for any surgery, thoracic or general, that I did. There were no untoward results, untoward deaths or preventable deaths documented against me. The overwhelming number of my patients stood in support of me and rallied round me. My office gathered 6000 signatures of people who stated they wanted me back at the hospital, and indeed, around the country people claimed I had twice that number.

The events seem to have started when my sole competitor, Dr. Mosca, began to badmouth me both to patients and other doctors. He also was reported to have said that he would never report to a black head of surgery. Subsequently, his partner was appointed to the position of head of surgery. This new head of surgery allegedly was informed by the President of the Board of Trustees that there was a problem in the thoracic and vascular section and that the new director should investigate my work. The chief did a retrospective study that reached back into December to pick up at least one of my cases. It was not clear whether he picked up cases from any other surgeons, which would have meant discrimination against me. In any case, contrary to hospital regulations, he did not establish any criteria for the review. Typically, when a hospital reviews a section, there is a full horizontal audit of all cases, which means all aortic studies, all carotid studies, and all surgeries, not just the surgeries of a single physician.

By that time, my practice was large and successful; I had built an office to serve my patients. I was in the process of building a Medical Mall that would serve Rockland County with a day surgery facility that would of course be in competition with the local hospitals and would give many surgeons a convenient and up to date facility for serving the growing population. I was an economic threat. My practice included many celebrity patients from both the black and white communities.

Dr. Glasser, the chief, stated that he spent six hundred hours going over every single case of surgery and every surgeon for a six-month period, January to June, 1985. He reviewed, according to him, two hundred twenty-two cases, and he alone created supporting minutes that he claimed he brought to our monthly surgical meetings, though in fact the cases never came to those meetings. Neither did he bring his minutes to the surgeons for correction or approval. By this means, he attempted to show that I had an opportunity to defend my surgical decisions, when in fact I did not even know a review was taking place. On this basis he attempted to show that I was incompetent, incorrigible, uneducable and a threat to life and limb, even though my results were excellent, and no cases of malpractice had been brought against me. I first learned of the findings of this review in mid-February 1987, twenty-seven months after the "review" began and twenty-one months after the review ended. During this period, no one informed me that I had done any surgery that was a threat to life and limb that warranted summary suspension of my privileges in thoracic and vascular surgery.

Later, two other chiefs of surgery testified that Dr. Glasser bragged about how he was personally getting me through his charts and the minutes of the section meeting. In fact, the rules and regulations of the hospital required Dr. Glasser to come to me personally and speak to me physician to physician about what he was finding in my charts and to tell me directly that I was a threat to life and limb. If he thought I was not rendering even minimum professional care, he had a moral obligation to come and talk to me. He had moreover a duty to come into my surgical room and observe and supervise. He did not do this because in fact I had no problems that required supervision or consulting. Equally troubling was the fact that at no step along this path did the legal counsel of the hospital, the president of the Board of Trustees, the administrator, the president of the medical staff, the chairman of the medical executive committee, the chief of the department of surgery, or the chairman of credentials speak to me about the review being anything but educational. None of these people answered my letters of inquiry when I found out about the review. No one but Dr. Glasser reviewed any of my cases. Everyone else simply reviewed his conclusions. I was moreover denied access to the 220 charts.

I gradually discovered that in some instances, my surgical charts and records had been sent out of the hospital for examination without notifying either me or my patients. Equally troubling, only my cases had been sent out of the hospital, indicating that this review was focused on me, not on other surgeons in the section. Sending out charts was a violation of hospital by-laws and state public health laws. When I was able to access this "review," I found that it contained no specifics, merely charts indicating categories such as technique, performance, skill and charting. All of these were considered deficient, though no specific evidence from cases was provided. One other doctor read the report. That doctor did not review any of the cases. Instead, I was told by another surgeon that when he met Dr. Glasser at another medical center, he was later told by a nurse in that surgical unit that Dr. Glasser bragged that he was the only chest surgeon in Rockland County, and that though I was well-trained, he was going to run me out of practice.

Subsequently, when I asked how I could "improve" if my performance was so poor, Dr. Glasser said he could not tell me. When pressed for an external review, Dr. Glasser chose to send seventeen of my cases to a surgeon whose specialty was treating varicose veins of celebrities, a surgeon who did not practice cardio-thoracic surgery at all. What I discovered was that the physicians to whom Dr. Glasser turned for review were trained together and had worked together. No truly outside, impartial expert was consulted. As this drama unfolded, my attorneys and I made an effort to discover the details of the review process, especially the scope of the review of surgeons and the development and approval of precise criteria that were to be used for measuring performance, since all I was told by one subsequent review by a friend of Dr. Glasser was that four of my cases were considered in some unspecified way substandard. Judge Walsh asked for clarification. Judge Carolyn Simon asked for clarification. Mr. Volte from the White Plains law firm asked for clarification about the criteria that were used or a clear set of criteria that might be used and agreed upon. Dr. Glasser and the hospital's attorney refused to reply to these letters.

Before I was notified that my privileges had been suspended, the hospital's credentials committee met for a few minutes to review Dr. Glasser's report. The committee structure at the hospital was a system of interlinking or overlapping committees, staffed for the most part by the same doctors, so that decisions made by one committee were unlikely to be questioned or challenged by any other committee. The public was told that thirty-nine doctors voted on my case, though in fact the thirty-nine committee members were just nine people who served on multiple committees plus a group of six external physicians who referred cases exclusively to my competitors. Perhaps two of the members of the committees were impartial, though I was unable to determine that with precision or to weigh the difficulty those two may have faced in the presence of such a unified front against me. In my previous experience on the credentials committees at Nyack and other hospitals, I knew that when doctors' performance was questioned, they always had an opportunity to speak to the committee and defend their practices. Both sides were heard from. In my case, however, I was not invited to meet with the credentials committee and heard about their decision only after the fact.

The reason that I was no longer on the Nyack credentials committee is critical to understanding my case and the totality of my career. Dr. Kalvert, the chair of the committee, had asked me if I was going to vote to close the Medical Staff to new physicians. I told him that as a black person, so many things had been closed to me that I could not possibly vote to close the doors on any qualified physician. I was not reappointed to the committee.

The credentials committee then took away my credentials in thoracic and vascular surgery on the recommendation of the chief of the department and the chief of the section. The chief of pacemaker surgery requested that my privileges remain intact, but those were taken away as well. Later I learned from a lawyer that Dr. Glasser had not attacked my pacemaker privileges because those charts had not been investigated, but he was sure that if he had examined my pacemaker charts, those would be bad as well. This merely proved that the seven members of the committee exercised absolute power and believed they could do whatever they wished. Those members of the credentials committee then reconvened as the executive committee of the hospital, and once again I was not asked to appear to defend my practice. Astoundingly, my general surgery credentials were untouched, so apparently in the judgment of these committees I was a danger to patients' life and limb only in those areas where I was in competition with their practices. After I eventually filed suit against the hospital, however, I was barred from the entire facility. There was only one person in the Credentials Committee who spoke about fairness and equitable treatment, and that was Dr. Paul Mercurio, who voiced the opinion that Dr. Johnson should be spoken to by the committee, and yet his name is not even mentioned in the minutes of the meeting. He was there, and he raised the issue. "Why not speak to Dr. Johnson about this and give him a chance to defend himself against the accusations that are being made?" That was not done.

Ten days after these committees met, there was a meeting of the Peer Review Committee, whose sole function was to determine whether the investigation of my surgical practice should continue. I was allowed to speak before this committee to explain what I felt was happening to my twenty-two-year medical career that had been questioned by people who were in direct competition with me. To this committee I admitted that I did not always have my charts completed on time, which was a legitimate finding about four of my cases, four out of the 222 that were supposedly reviewed. At no time however had those delays constitute infractions of the hospital by-laws. This committee consisted of the same people who served on the other committees.

I came to that meeting early and sat down. I was reading the paper, waiting for them to come in. When the members arrived, Dr. Winikoff called the meeting to order and proceeded to give the committee members fifteen minutes to read the six-month investigative report that was 46 pages long. When the fifteen minutes was over, they attempted to put an end to my 22-year career, despite the fact that I had no malpractice cases, no wrongful deaths, and good results in all but a few cases. In cases that were questionable, I was absolutely ready to defend my clinical decisions. I had brought a basketball bag full of literature, periodicals, textbooks, and reports from other physicians who had defended my procedures and my care for patients. When I began to explain what had happened and how I believed the report was flawed, and that the process was flawed in regard to hospital rules, civil rights, the lack of approved committee minutes, and constitutional rights, the committee did not wish to listen.

At the Peer Review committee meeting, I was allowed to explain one case in which I was charged with providing incomplete records. I explained that the chart had been tampered with and that I was able to recover the missing documents only after working with the primary physician. Moreover, some of the pertinent items were at the Montefiore Hospital. Then Dr. Young stood up and said that he could not stay and listen to an explanation of every case, so he was leaving. During the meeting it was discovered that Dr. Glasser had not dictated meeting minutes in a timely manner, that he was six months behind in dictations, that he had sent charts out of the hospital against the rules, that he had not spoken to me in violation of the rules, that he had been the only person to review my 222 charts, that outsider reviewers chosen by him had reviewed only 25 cases and mine alone, not any cases performed by other doctors. He admitted that no reviews had been done by the pro-quality assurance team, and he was not specific about what constituted in his opinion major and minor deficiencies in each case. When Dr. Winikoff, the chair of the committee, asked Glasser how he came to his conclusions, he said he had taken 600 hours to review my cases. He never said that he had talked to me, visited one of my surgeries, or watched me operate.

None of my explanations of charting, about my charting not violating the rules and regulations of the hospital, or Dr. Winikoff's statement about my competence to do charts were noted in the minutes of that meeting. Neither was Dr. Young's statement that he was leaving because he did not have time to listen to a discussion of every one of my charts. In fact, the minutes were never brought back to the committee for approval.

After this travesty, a group of concerned citizens went to the hospital to discuss with Mr. Dawson the suspension of my privileges in thoracic and vascular surgery, and Mr. Dawson made several grossly inaccurate statements about the suspension, the process, and the quality of the review process. He said to the concerned citizens who had rallied around me that he was concerned about my deaths and that I had preventable deaths. The fact was that he had never mentioned preventable deaths, and that charge was never among those made by Dr. Glasser or sustained by any of the committees. If there had been any such deaths, they should have been named, and names were never brought forward. Moreover, if this was a genuine concern, it should have been brought forward immediately in a review, not mentioned long after the completion of a twenty-seven month process, because if in fact I had preventable deaths it would have been immoral to allow me to continue surgery without pointing out my errors. Mr. Dawson claimed that I had been informally notified about the case review all along, and that I was only formally notified after my privileges had been suspended. As for the cases themselves, it was years until I learned which cases had been selected by Dr. Glasser for review.

Later I learned that Dr. Glasser, Mr. Dawson and others had met privately and decided not to use the legally acceptable methods of review, which would have required them to notify the professional review organization for our area and have them investigate. Instead, they deliberately chose to go after my privileges, as their own attorney later informed us at a meeting in White Plains, and to hire outside reviewers of their own choice.

As for the issue of racial prejudice, I had brought to Mr. Dawson letters that demonstrated how one doctor in the surgical area was bigoted. Mr. Dawson's response to me at that time was to say that "You people are treated like this all over the world. If you think you can be treated better somewhere else, you should go there." In response to questions from the NAACP, Mr. Dawson said he could not talk about many issues, because they were being discussed by other attorneys.

After these events, I began to have difficulty with my malpractice insurance company. Without notification, the company cancelled my insurance for a period. When the company told the hospital I was no longer insured, the hospital then revoked my rights to be on the hospital grounds or even to visit my own patients who were already in Nyack Hospital. Signs were posted at every nursing station. Meanwhile, Good Samaritan Hospital in New York also suspended my privileges, though the two major hospitals where I worked in New Jersey would have nothing to do with these processes and kept me in good standing.

None of this should have been a surprise to me, based on my previous experience of racism and of institutional racism. There is a difference, however, between what people are prepared to say compared to what they will actually do, and I was struck throughout by the silent power of institutionalized racism, the capacity of a group of people who share one heritage to support each other even when one of their number is carrying out an act that is on the face of it illegal, immoral and likely to backfire if it is done to a person of character and strength. How is it that the others engage in silent complicity? I recalled one specific occasion when I asked Dr. Mosca to come help me. I had an abdominal aortic aneurysm, and I thought his opinion would be beneficial. He refused to come, saying that the patient would probably die anyway, that he was not teaching, that I was his competitor, and there was nothing he was going to do for me. This was very early in my training at the hospital. At about the same time one of my friends was at a meeting in Florida and bumped into a surgeon who had been thrown out of the Montefiore training program. At that time this doctor had finished his training elsewhere and was a partner of Dr. Mosca. The doctor told my friend that Dr. Mosca had commented that I had come into the county, but I was not going to stay long because they were going to run this black bastard out of town. They also claimed that all of my patients were dying. This same friend went and spoke to Haskel Cohen, the writer for Parade Magazine who got me the scholarship to Duquesne and reported the same story.

My career as a heart surgeon was initially boosted by my willingness to work anywhere at any hours. The first real vascular case I had was a ruptured abdominal aortic aneurysm in the middle of the night. I did the case with the help of a urologist and a general practitioner who was also a general surgeon. The patient lived another seven years. He was the president of American Cyanamid, and with that successful surgery, people in the community began to feel that I could really take care of them, and they began to come to me in large numbers. In another instance, I had a patient from a car accident in the E.R. who was in profound shock from a ruptured spleen. I could not get any surgeons to operate with me, so I finally found an orthopedic surgeon who came into the O.R. and we did a splenectomy together. This was the situation I worked in during the first few years at Nyack Hospital. Moreover, no matter what surgery I did, at the surgical meetings, I was always forced to present my emergency room cases, even if there were far more appropriate cases to study that were of more educational value. This was done in order to show that I had mortalities. Literally over fourteen years at that hospital, thousands of cases that would have been more appropriately studied were not presented in order to paint a picture that my surgery was bad or that I had bad results. If a patient had been run over by a bus that then backed over him, so that he came in more dead than alive, that was the kind of case that was selected for me to present.

Nonetheless, by doing these critical cases in the emergency room, my skills sharpened. Many people began to live who would have died, and that heightened my reputation in the community. Still, I was denied upward mobility at the Nyack Hospital. In response, I reached out to the Board of Health and became the Vice President and President. I continued to make house calls in the community and to be on the St. Dominic's Advisory Board, the Rockland County Red Cross board, and a participant in scholarships. I spoke at high schools, synagogues, churches and West Point. I also became the Haverstraw police and fire department surgeon. In other words, I carved out a life outside the hospital of service to the community. But in the Nyack Hospital itself, over fourteen years there was one battle after another, and whomever became chief of the vascular section set out immediately to see if they could cut back on the number of patients I was seeing and to discredit the work I was doing and to defame me as much as possible. There was a constant whispering campaign that came back to me from reports by nurses and by way of other doctors who eventually came around to think it was fun to let me know that I was not liked and was not wanted in the community by some of the doctors.

I filed a complaint against one doctor who seemed even to have gone to the length of failing to intubate one of my patients who needed emergency care. I had not directly asked him to do the procedure, because I was on call at another hospital, but that doctor was on call at Nyack and had a responsibility to perform that procedure. I took that story to the hospital attorney, Mr. Dawson, who asked me to document my concern. I brought a number of letters that had been written to a previous peer review committee. There were upwards of 20 letters from doctors, nurses and technicians who wrote that this doctor was often inappropriate in his speech and actions, and that he was prejudiced and bigoted. Mr. Dawson's response was that if that doctor was a problem, then his whole department was a problem. He told me it was I who represented a disruptive force, and it was then that he said to me, "All you people (black people) are treated the same around the world, and if you think that you can be treated better someplace else, then you should go there." I went to the head of the department, and he said he did not believe there was a racial problem. He said that he had grown up in a household where his parents would take him to the zoo, and when they got to the monkey cage, his parents would say, "Look at all the niggers." He said his parents were still good people. He said he himself was a fair and even-handed person, so it didn't really matter what that bigoted doctor was doing, because he was good at his work, and he hoped that I could understand and function around it. The other vascular surgeons, however, continued to pressure the head of the department to get rid of me because I had not done enough supervised surgery, even though the other doctors refused to provide any supervision.

Back in 1975 and 1976, Dr. Mosca pushed to have a vertical audit of just my cases. Because of the racial climate, particularly involving Dr. Mosca, I was hesitant to comply. I went to Judge Caroline K. Simon, who pointed out that the Joint Commission on Accreditation of Hospitals did not permit this kind of audit without sitting down prior to the audit and establishing criteria that would permit all parties to know what kind of information and evaluation was being sought. That was never done. I made that point on several occasions when others proposed that my work alone be audited, especially on the occasion of the review that led to the suspension of my privileges. From the perspective of many of the doctors, and of Dr. Mosca in particular, I was an enemy by the fact of my existence. I was a black person, and worse than being a black person, I was a successful black person, and worse than that, I had gotten a residency at Montefiore Hospital when there were 400 applicants for two places in cardiac surgery, and I had been successful in the residency. I had become a chief in that program and was completely trained in cardiac and thoracic surgery, which was unusual for an American black in our country. There were only four other black cardio-thoracic surgeons in the entire United States. All of that was already strange and threatening, and to have me come into the Rockland area and operate on the president of American Cyanimide and have him live and have him going about getting patients for me was too much. My patients included Harry Bellaver, the actor from Naked City, a popular television detective series; Myron Cohen, the comedian from the Ed Sullivan show; and Helen Hayes, the first lady of the theater. I had a practice that was 96% white patients, which was very disturbing to many of the doctors. Moreover, I was married to a member of the Sulzberger family who owned the New York Times, and my wife was a white lady. None of that helped my situation in the hospital.

Once, the chief in his infinite wisdom pushed me into a locker when we were discussing the value of keeping a wet lung syndrome completely dry. Our views differed. It was my judgment that a person with wet lung should be given enough fluid to allow the kidneys to function and put out 30–50 cc per hour. Otherwise, we would run into renal problems, especially with the type of antibiotics that we were asking the kidneys to handle. Because I had the audacity to make that statement, I was told, "Look, you people have to start from the bottom. You can't just come into a place and jump on the top. That's what's wrong with you people."

Had I not worked my way from the bottom?

The other key member of the operating room was the head nurse, who had worked in the Army Nursing Corps, very much like a M.A.S.H. unit. Unfortunately, she was bigoted in her treatment of me. One day she called me a "boy" in front of at least one other nurse who could document it. "Listen, boy, you have to get your ass in here on time!" Whenever she could do it, she bumped my cases to the end of the schedule. Other doctors were allowed to call in to schedule their cases, and one of the doctors routinely came in after me and added his name ahead of mine on the schedule.

Mr. Dawson was a problem in other ways. Once I was invited down to give a speech about my career because I had been selected for a humanitarian award by the B'nai B'rith of New York City. At the same time I had been selected as one of the hundred most distinguished graduates in the first one hundred years of Duquesne University, as well as one of the 50 most distinguished graduates in the first fifty years of Dwight Morrow High School in Englewood. The volunteers at the hospital were impressed by my accomplishments, none of which were allowed to be published in the Nyack Hospital paper. Mr. Dawson came down and heard me speak to the volunteers, said that he was impressed by my speaking, and then declared that I should not be allowed to teach the nurses or paramedics in the hospital. The only reason I can imagine is that he did not want me to be more popular there. He also did not allow publication of more common awards like being president of the Board of Health, or medical director of the Hillcrest Nursing Home, or Chief of Surgery at the Community Hospital. I was not allowed to be on any of the important committees, except for that year when I declined to vote against allowing others to join the staff, which was another transparent move to avoid competition.

Sometime after Mr. Dawson spoke to me about my going someplace else if I thought I could do better, he came and asked me to give $25,000 to the hospital. The hospital was running a building fund, and as I was one of the busiest people in the hospital, the organizers felt I should give that much. I reminded him that I could not, in good conscience, give any money to the hospital because I was upset at the rumors being bandied about that a building fund was being established with the commitment to give ten cents out of every dollar to the fund raisers.

When I refused to donate to the building fund, the hospital sent another doctor to me to ask me to give. I declined with the same reasons, pointing out in addition the bigotry of some of the people in charge of the hospital. After a while, just to annoy them, I leased a Rolls Royce and parked it in front of the hospital. Then a member of the board wrote to me that if I could afford to have a Rolls Royce, I could afford to give something to the hospital. Again, I explained that money wasn't the reason I declined to give to the fund. It was because of how the hospital treated me, and by extension my patients. I was upset at the stories of deals that were circulating, stories that needed to be investigated. One such new rumor concerned the way finances were abused in setting up the Nyack Hospital Medi-Stop at the Helen Hayes Hospital. Other rumors concerned property purchases and land speculation.

Next Mr. Dawson came to tell me that the hospital was going to establish a physician rating system, and this was confirmed when I spoke with the president of the Board of Health, who explained to a staff meeting that doctors who gave money to the hospital as well as doctors who sent patients home early or helped the hospital in other ways that would raise revenue would get higher ratings. The higher the rating, the more the hospital would be able to help support that physician. The way the hospital could help doctors including prioritizing access to the operating rooms and appointing doctors to important committees. The hospital was also starting a referral service. The referral service would provide three names of good doctors when people called for referrals for different kinds of medical problems.

Now there were about 200 doctors in the hospital, and every specialty had more than three doctors, so those who donated or increased hospital revenue would get more patients and more income. The hospital also set up an HMO for its own employees, and only doctors chosen by the hospital could be used by those employees. I became concerned when I encountered patients who needed care at home. People were being sent home who were not street ready.

Mr. Dawson was even more upset by my plans to start a Medical Mall. My initial plan was to open a one-day hospital, but pressure was placed on me to abandon that idea, which competed with Nyack's one-day surgery center. The Medical Mall, which was eventually built and was a great success, was designed to house twenty-two different medical disciplines, with 76 doctors participating in a rotating, time-sharing doctor's facility that had procedure rooms for the kinds of outpatient surgery that all of us did in our offices. We projected saving insurance companies between $400 to $2000 per case. The hospital saw this as a tremendous threat, just as the doctors saw a house call service as a threat to their hospital-based care. Those were all reasons why I was targeted.

In February 1990, I filed an antitrust case against Nyack Hospital in the Southern District of New York. In September 1991, that case was dismissed for failure to exhaust administrative remedies. Eventually, the legal cases over a ten-year period filled thirty-five banker boxes. The decision of the Southern District was affirmed by the U.S. Court of Appeals for the Second Circuit. The Circuit held that I needed to go to the New York Public Health Council (PHC) before I could seek redress in federal court. While my case was pending in the Second Circuit, the New York State Office of Professional Medical Conduct (OPMC) brought charges against me seeking revocation of my license. These charges were based on materials supplied to OPMC by Nyack Hospital.

A three-member panel of the OPMC found that Nyack Hospital's revocation of my privileges was not based on any quality assurance concerns, but rather that the "entire study abrogated the principles of quality improvement and reduced it to a punitive retrospective exercise." The OPMC Hearing Committee's concern went beyond the process of Nyack Hospital's suspension of my privileges, questioning "the credibility of the surgeon in charge of the section who ran the Quality Assurance Program" as well. The OPMC Hearing Committee detailed four specific pages of criticism of the Nyack Hospital process and the charges which were made against me.

In January of 1993, six years into this ordeal, the OPMC rendered its final decision and exonerated me of virtually all of the forty-one charges brought against me, except for all but two and part of one minor charge.

The OPMC Hearing committee found that suspension of my license was not warranted. Instead, the OPMC Hearing Committee only ordered that I complete 50 hours of education over the next two years, consisting of 25 hours each in thoracic and vascular surgery. By January 1994 I had completed over 86.75 hours of education, well above what was required by the OPMC. By letter dated March 4, 1994, the OPMC acknowledged that I had met all that was required of me and that no further action by the OPMC was required.

The press release issued following the Panel's findings is worth quoting in part:

"State Hearing Panel Finds no Evidence to Suspend or Revoke Dr. Fletcher Johnson's License.

State Panel's Findings After Twenty Days of Hearings Do Not Support 1987 Action Taken Against Dr. Johnson by Nyack Hospital."

"Two world renowned surgeons testified as experts on Dr. Johnson's behalf. The first was Dr. George Reed, Chief of Cardiothoracic Surgery and President of the Medical Staff and Professor of Surgery at New York Medical College at the Westchester County Medical Center. Dr. Reed testified that Dr. Johnson had handled properly all four of the thoracic cases which were at issue and that one was handled "superbly." He testified further that he felt he felt that 'a terrible injustice had been done' to Dr. Johnson in bringing the charges. Dr. Reed testified further that Dr. Johnson's case reflected 'the hallmark of a good surgeon and a very decent person.'

"The second expert witness who testified for Dr. Johnson on the four vascular cases was Dr. Frank J. Veith, Chief of Vascular Surgery at Montefiore Medical Center and Albert Einstein College of Medicine in the Bronx and Professor and Past Chairman of the Department of Surgery at both of those teaching hospitals. For 15 years Dr. Veith has chaired the annual Montefiore/Einstein vascular symposium which is attended annually by more than 1000 vascular surgeons. Dr. Veith fully supported Dr. Johnson, and testified that he felt 'there is some gross injustice' in trying to make judgments against Dr. Johnson based on the facts he saw."

"Among the physicians testifying for Dr. Johnson were: the former president of the Rockland County Medical Society who testified that 'decisions [at Nyack Hospital] were carried out without any type of medial input of medical knowledge' and that he did not believe that the decision to revoke Dr. Johnson's privileges was made for 'a surgical or technical reason.' As he testified, Dr. Johnson was never given the chance at Nyack to explain the surgery he had performed prior to the revocation of his privileges. Another physician who testified was a former president of the Nyack Hospital medical staff and former chairman of its medical executive committee, who testified to Dr. Johnson's excellent treatment of one of his patients whom Nyack and the State charged was treated in a substandard fashion. This doctor testified that Dr. Johnson's problems at Nyack began with a 'personal vendetta' against him by another physician. Also testifying on Dr. Johnson's behalf was another former chairman of the Department of Surgery at Nyack and former president of the Nyack Hospital medical staff and chief of the surgery section."

"In contrast to the 41-page decision of the Hearing Panel after 20 days of sworn testimony, Nyack had conducted a one-day 'hearing' in 1987, at which no witnesses were placed under oath and at which no evidence was introduced. This resulted in a one-paragraph finding, without explanation, against Dr. Johnson."

The right to discovery is essential to coming to any kind of conclusion in this kind of case, which in fact was nothing but a grand scheme motivated by greed, hate, bigotry, and total disregard for the results that were obtained. The one undeniable reason for the investigation was to get rid of Dr. Johnson. Only my cases were selected to be sent out of the hospital. The only person inside the hospital who reviewed any cases was Dr. Glasser, who was in complete conflict of interest. The hospital administration had lost four prior civil rights cases, which demonstrated its hate and bias and the type of climate that was allowed to exist at the hospital.

Eventually the Public Health Committee (PHC) met to consider my complaint, on July 29, 1994. In a letter dated September 7, 1994, the PHC stated that although concerns were raised about whether I was afforded due process when Nyack Hospital revoked my privileges, there were not sufficient votes to either credit or discredit my complaint. The PHC letter further stated that the PHC would take no further action in this case. So the OPMC review could conclude that there was evidence of a vendetta, repudiate the charges, and point in wonder to the fact that Nyack Hospital had held a one hour meeting to decide my fate, without allowing me to state my case, and then the PHC could conclude there wasn't sufficient evidence that there was a lack of due process. Once again the system worked to protect itself and to avoid discord, even if it meant offering no justice.

On or about October 14, 1994, I filed a second complaint in the Southern District of New York (1994 Action, Civil Action No.94.7464). In this 1994 action, I brought claims against Nyack Hospital and others for antitrust violations under Sections 1 and 2 of the Sherman Act, tortious interference with contract, and violations of the federal civil rights laws, specifically 42 U.S.C. ss 1981 and 1985(3). By an order dated June 27, 1995, the Southern District of New York granted Defendant's Motion for Summary Judgment on the Antitrust and tortious interference claims which related to the 1987 revocation of my thoracic and vascular privileges. The court reasoned that by the time that I cleared myself at the OPMC and then filed a complaint with the PHC, the statute of limitations had run and these claims were therefore time barred. To put this in plainer English, I had filed a complaint with the PHC years before, only to be told I had to wait until I had exhausted all administrative remedies. When I finally won in the course of those administrative remedies, I was then told it was now too late to file that complaint again, because the statute of limitations on the offenses had expired. This is law, but it is not justice.

With respect to the civil rights claims, however, which sought relief with respect to the events that surrounded my 1994 request for extension of my privileges, the court stayed my claims pending resort to the Public Health Committee. That complaint was credited in my behalf. Nyack Hospital was directed to review its actions. Curiously and importantly, in its letter reporting its "determination," this time the PHC, which had in 1994 found no sufficient grounds to find a denial of due process, used the following language to describe what had been done to me: "The Public Health Council finds that the actions taken by Nyack Hospital in denying Dr. Fletcher Johnson's application for reinstatement of privileges in vascular and thoracic surgery, when considered in their totality, are sufficiently lacking in fairness as to constitute bad faith." This supports the finding of the OPMC that "the case against Dr. Johnson represented by the charges and selected testimony of its witnesses did not meet the standards of objectivity and candor." And that finding was consistent with the thoughtful support offered by the May 1987 NAACP investigation, which found that during the 27 month investigation, "no effort was made. . .to give him fair notice or an opportunity to correct so-called deficiencies, not of which were ever defined or proven." Ten years of administrative and court actions to overturn a single paragraph written February 10, 1987, in bad faith, based on the greed and bigotry of a competitor, and supported by a small committee of like minded individuals or people too craven to protest an injustice:

"The Medical Executive Committee [of Nyack Hospital], at its meeting of February 10, 1987, voted to approve the recommendation of the Credentials Committee that your privileges to perform thoracic and vascular surgery, inclusive of pacemaker privileges, be rescinded. Your privileges in general surgery are not affected by this action. . . .

These actions have been taken because the Medical Executive Committee has determined based on the information currently before it, your work in thoracic and vascular surgery does not meet standards acceptable to Nyack Hospital."

A federal court date was set for June 1997, some ten years after this personal trial began, and an out of court settlement was reached in May 1997. It was agreed that the terms of the settlement would be undisclosed and confidential. I have respected those terms. I can, however, restate the issues in plain English. The delays of the administrative system denied me the right to pursue all my claims. Civil rights, law, however, allowed me to exert sufficient leverage to attain a settlement. It is typical for institutions, in such cases, to do all they can to protect their reputations by insisting upon undisclosed and confidential settlements. I was not afforded the same benefit when my reputation was damaged; more important, my patients and the patients I might have served well over that ten year period in the State of New York were not given any consideration whatsoever, just as their health had not been considered by those who wanted to limit the number of cardio-thoracic surgeons in the county so that they could reap the monetary rewards, in spite of serious questions about their capacity to perform the operations from which they derived their income. Neither were the physicians or the Hospital required to face the underlying racism that contributed to this debacle.

Invictus

Good Samaritan Hospital in New York withdrew my privileges shortly after Nyack Hospital did so. The agreement was that Good Samaritan would abide by any settlement with Nyack. After my privileges were restored at both hospitals, however, Good Samaritan did not follow through with its pledge to hold a Fair Hearing to clear my name. The attorneys for Dr. Glasser and his associates continued to pursue me in order to protect their own reputations after they were shown in court to have carried out a sham evaluation and the hospital had been forced to settle. In response to Good Samaritan's delays, which were prompted by a letter from Dr. Glasser's lawyers that repeated all the charges that had been repudiated by the State hearing panel, I corresponded with the Executive Director of the New York State Department of Health. The edited letter quoted here may stand as my conclusion to the affair and my comment on the struggles I have faced, which have not shaken the faith and convictions I have expressed throughout this autobiography.

> Dear Ms. Westervelt:
>
> I thank you for answering my letter of April 20, 1998 in a timely fashion.
>
> I assure you that the information in my letter is amply contained in my Verified Complaint. What I sent you is a synopsis, a clarification, and often a guide as to where in the voluminous material sent by myself and by Good Samaritan Hospital—the facts—the truth—can be documented.
>
> I can only pray this letter does not anger, does not irritate, or appear argumentative to you. As seekers of fact and truth, you need facts, truths and the whole story. To draw a correct conclusion, you need truthful premises.
>
> I am sure that this material going back over 11 years is frustrating to you. I can only hope you have the courage to read the

material. In actuality, I can assure you that this is a simple case. It is a case where someone and some institutions got together to lie about someone knowing that that lie would destroy that person in his area of expertise and thus destroy him economically, eliminate his practice, and preclude him from building a medical mall; thereby they would establish a monopoly and benefit enormously economically.

It took ten years to prove that the initial review of my work was a complete sham. It took that long before I was able to get the appropriate records from Nyack Hospital. Even then, the hospital was unable to find all 222 charts. They came up with 187.

Nevertheless, within seven to ten days of reading these charts, it was clear that a double standard was used to eliminate me, and that Dr. Glasser had shielded himself and his partners from meaningful scrutiny.

Dr. Glasser's statistical review could not be reproduced and was clearly bogus. Within the month of that proof, Nyack Hospital settled with me.

Now it is more than one year, and Good Samaritan Hospital has withheld my name-clearing Fair Hearing Plan, which we both agreed would happen when I requested it and I had settled with Nyack. In this agreement between myself and Good Samaritan Hospital, there was no provision that if they gave me back my privileges, there would be no Fair Hearing, nor was our agreement contingent on the type of settlement that I made with Nyack Hospital.

I am frustrated that for over 10 long years the people of Rockland County were deprived of my services; my referring physicians in Rockland County were deprived of my services. . .my patients, my children, my wife and I unfairly suffered.

I have been able to survive, especially mentally, because I am a true believer in Jesus Christ, our Lord. I use the Bible—Second Corinthians, 4th chapter, 8th and 9th verses:

"We are troubled on every side, yet not distressed. We are perplexed, but not in despair. Persecuted, but not forsaken. Cast down, but not destroyed."

Then, there is that old Negro spiritual called "The Solid Rock." The refrain goes:

On Christ, the solid Rock I stand. All other ground is sinking sand, All other ground is sinking sand.

There is a poem that personifies me, that is a poem by William Ernest Henley that is called "Invictus."

Having studied pharmacy at the University of Bologna in Bologna, Italy, in Italian, I found that the word INVICTUS comes from the Latin and means "invincible," and the Latin word "vincere," which means to conquer. To "win" comes from the word "invictus."

The poem goes, and I am sure you have heard it and will remember it:

Invictus
Out of the night that covers me,
Black as the Pit from pole to pole
I thank whatever gods may be
For my unconquerable soul.

In the fell clutch of circumstance
I have not winced, nor cried aloud.
Under the bludgeonings of chance
My head is bloodied, but unbowed.

Beyond this place of wrath and tears
Looms the terror of the shade,
And yet the menace of the years
Finds, and shall find me, unafraid.

It matters not how strait the gate,
How charged with punishments the scroll,
I am the master of my fate;
I am the captain of my soul.

God has chosen me to stand up to this injustice. Therefore I must make every effort to have a larger conversation, so that the people who unwittingly, and those who with full intention, purpose, and malice conspired to do this, will never again wantonly destroy the life of another human being.

Fletcher J. Johnson, M.D., F.A.C.S.

Made in the USA
Coppell, TX
23 June 2021

57931598R00098